ANOTHER CHANCE

YOUR *Life* IS NOT OVER

CHRISTOPHER EVANS

Christopher Evans

Another Chance - Your Life Is Not Over
Copyright © 2017 Christopher Evans
Evans Publications
190 Industrial Drive
Hogansville, Georgia 30230

All rights reserved. No part of this book may be reproduced (except for inclusion in reviews), disseminated or utilized in any form or by any means, electronic or mechanical, including photocopying, recording, or in any information storage and re-trieval system, or the Internet/World Wide Web without written permission from the author or publisher.

Book design by:
Jody Mayfield
www.jodymayfield.com

Printed in the United States of America
Another Chance - Your Life Is Not Over
Christopher Evans
1. Another Chance 2. Christopher Evans 3. Inspirational
Library of Congress Control Number:
ISBN 13: 978-0-692-06660-7

ANOTHER CHANCE

CHRISTOPHER EVANS

Christopher Evans

Dedication
To my daughter Christa Evans
and my son Christopher Evans, II.

Christopher Evans

THANK YOU

Another Chance

First, I thank God for the wonderful privilege and the awesome purpose He has given me. He has blessed me with unusual and unique gifts and favored my ministry and for that, I am eternally grateful.

To my mother and best friend, thank you for being the best mom a son could have. You are truly one of God's best, and I will forever be indebted to you for the love, patience and prayers.

To my sister and brother-in-law, Jeanette and Jeff, thanks for being in my corner and believing in me. Thanks for all the cookouts and for eating all my food.

To Jerome Cofield, thanks for all the laughs, even though we were mainly laughing at me. You will never know how your friendship saved my life. Thanks man!!!

To Pastor Jesse Sanders, thanks for leading me to Christ and being patient with me as I went through the discipleship process. I would not have this wonderful relationship with Christ if it wasn't for you.

To Dr. P. Ronald Wilder, one of the best kept secrets in the body of Christ, thanks for never giving up on me. You have been with me through the highs and lows of life. Eagle, I am proud to say I have gotten myself together and I didn't lose my dignity. (Inside joke).

To Bishop Horace Smith, Bishop Flynn Johnson, and Bishop Wiley Jackson, thanks for the impartation. You guys have shaped me into the man I am today.

To Pastor Smokie and Carla Norful, I truly love you guys. Thanks for all the lunches and late night phone calls to motivate me to believe that "GREATER" was and is possible. I will never forget the conversations that caused me to believe that I was someone with worth and value. Pastor Norful, you didn't know you were encouraging me, because you were simply being who you are: a man who causes people to dream bigger than they thought possible. You are an awesome friend and brother and this is an opportunity for me to say "thank you."

To Bishop Dreyfus Smith, my big brother, thanks for coaching, confronting, and caring. You are the ultimate big brother and I am better for knowing you. Thanks for always listening, even when I was making no sense. Thank you Tonja for your willingness to allow me share some of the personal details of our life and marriage. You are truly a class act and I honestly appreciate you. I love and thank the "DESTINY" church family. You guys are the best church in the entire world and I am truly fortunate and grateful that God selected me to be your pastor. Thanks for your years of support and prayers. You are an incredible group of people.

To Mrs. Tina Brown and Mr. Jody Mayfield, I do not have the words to express my gratitude for the encouragement and inspiration that you all have given me. You caused me to believe in and experience the God of "Another Chance." Thanks for the calls, the prayers, and the motivation. You lifted me out of a state of confusion and depression and caused me to dream again. Through you, I gained the confidence to believe that my life was not over. I would have never guessed that Mrs. Latoya Parks and Ms. Shanitra Ramson would be the world greatest proofreading team. Thank you so much for your commitment to this project.

I could not have pulled this off without you. Finally, to my two favorite people in the whole world, Christa and Christopher II, you are the best kids a father could ask for and I love you more than anything. You have been the source of my drive and devotion. Thanks Christa for being daddy's girl and never allowing me to settle for less. You have always held me in the highest regard and you made it impossible for me to disappoint. CJ, you are a wonderful son and friend and through your words, I gained the courage to fight through every storm of life because I knew you were watching. Thanks your unending support.

Contents

Introduction: Another Chance 1

Chapter : There Is Still Hope 7

Chapter 2: Why Do We Make Bad Choices? 11

Chapter 3: The People In Your Life 23

Chapter 4: This Is Not A Sprint 33

Step 1 - Remember: God Loves You 39

Step 2 - Repent And Make It Right 47

Step 3 - Receive God's Forgiveness 65

Step 4 - Rededicate Your Life 75

Step 5 - Remove All Residue 83

Step 6 - Reestablish Foundational Principles 91

Step 7 - Refocus Your Life 101

Step 8 - Respect Boundaries 109

Step 9 - Refuse To Repeat Your Mistake 119

Step 10 - Rewrite Your Story 129

Step 11 - Realign With Your Purpose 137

Step 12 - Rehearse Your Success 145

Step 13 - Resume Your Life 151

Step 14 - Remain Diligent 159

Conclusion 165

INTRODUCTION
ANOTHER CHANCE

It was two o'clock in the morning, and so far I had not been able to sleep a wink. All sorts of thoughts were piercing my mind as I lay in the smelly and dilapidated motel room. My flesh crawled as I thought about the drug dealers and prostitutes who were right outside my door, hovering around the place like vultures over dying prey. I feared for my life as the darkness enveloped the room like in a creepy horror film.

For the past several years, I hadn't stayed anywhere but four or five-star hotels, so to find myself in an environment of this caliber was too much to bear. Were the days of lavish décor, valet parking, and beautiful views gone? Was this place a glimpse into my future reality? As I lay there, one thought penetrated my mind: could I lose everything I'd worked so hard to gain? Anxiety and emotions churned within me. I had never experienced pain like that before.

After fifteen years of marriage, I had to face the harsh reality that my wife and I were getting a divorce, and I had the dreadful task of telling my congregation about it the following day. I had to face the people who trusted and depended on me. Divorce is such an ugly word, and I was ashamed that it had to come out of my mouth. I'd played the scenario out a thousand times in my mind, and still I found no easy way to break the news.

Many questions came to me. What was going to happen to my church? What was going to happen to my life? What was going to happen to my name and my reputation?

Through all the pondering and contemplation, I was completely oblivious of the time. Just then, light shone through the curtain and I realized it was daybreak. I got up and looked into the bathroom mirror. I looked like a hundred miles of bad road. My eyes were red and puffy from the lack of sleep. To be honest, at that moment I didn't even recognize myself. This wasn't the Chris Evans I knew. I felt like I was in the middle of a horrible nightmare, and I wished someone would just wake me up.

My mental state was also in disarray as anguish and confusion ran rampant in my mind. I felt in no condition to make this enormous announcement. I pictured my congregation responding in outrage and displeasure. I tried to shake the negative thoughts and think along positive lines: They loved me, right? I mean, I trusted these people with my life. They would never do anything to hurt me.

I practiced my speech, making every effort not to have an emotional breakdown. Regardless of how hard I tried, I could not escape the tears. My heart weighed a ton; I felt like my body had been hit by a train, and the anxiety started all over again. I was having last-minute thoughts of maybe not attending the service, but I couldn't run from it forever. I loved these people, and they deserved to know the truth from their pastor.

Why was this so difficult? I guess I was feeling more vulnerable than I'd ever felt in my life. I felt like I was at the mercy not only of God but of the people. I felt like they held my fate in their hands. As I continued to look into the mirror, I asked myself, "How many real relationships do I have? How many real friends do I have? Who can love me through this condition? Who can love me through this situation?"

I had spent the majority of my life encouraging and loving people, but at that moment, I really needed someone to love and encourage me. Above everything else, I'd invested so much stock in the covenant of marriage. I felt like a complete failure. I felt like my life and my ministry were over. What could I say to my congregation? How could I minister when the Bible and society make family the pinnacle of everything we do?

I looked at the clock and saw it was time for me to dress and head over to the church. My heart was racing like a horse coming into the homestretch at the Kentucky Derby. My eyes began to tear up again, and I had a sinking feeling in the pit of my stomach. I found myself crying and calling out to God to help me, to strengthen me, to give me the courage I needed to make it through this moment. I quoted every scripture I knew—anything that would give me hope and consolation.

While driving toward the church, everything was a blur. All I could think about was the inevitability of the moment I was about to face. It was like time was at a standstill. All I could hear was my heart beating as the fear and anxiety increased because I knew that in just a few minutes, my life was going to change forever.

As I approached the church, I saw all the cars and all the people. The place was full.

"Lord, do I really want to go through with this?" I asked myself as I entered the parking lot. The enemy took one last shot at my mind, and I felt less than a man. I felt like a moral failure, like I had misled or deceived people. I felt as though I was a poor excuse for a father, a pastor, and a husband. I even wondered what my wife was thinking or feeling at that moment and what thoughts were going through her mind, because she knew I was preparing to share a very personal matter with our congregation.

I managed to make it through praise and worship, and I prayed God would continue to give me strength. I was introduced, and I immediately began my sermon. As I was preaching, the only thought on my mind was that in about thirty minutes the room would be filled with overwhelming sadness.

I finished my message, and the service ended. After that, I asked the members to remain. I went to my green room and changed. I was there; I was at the point I'd dreaded all night long. I walked back into the church sanctuary and looked at my congregation.

I could sense that everybody knew something was wrong. I began to give my speech, which I had agonized over all night, and the moment I mentioned the words separation and divorce, I heard the cries of heartbroken people who were trying to grasp this emotional shock. As I was trying to hold it together, I told myself that life as I knew it was over.

As I exited the church, the moment seemed surreal. I thought the ride there had been difficult, but the ride home was even worse. I felt a small bit of relief since I had told my congregation, but now I could not help but wonder, "Will I have a church next week? Who will come? What are people saying? What about the people who have been antagonistic toward me? What are they feeling? What are they thinking?"

These are the kinds of thoughts people face when they have gone through some kind of catastrophic situation. It is in these moments of damage and great disturbance that we feel as if our lives are over and done.

The purpose of this book is to speak to the people who have faced, are facing, or will face devastating moments in their lives: moments like mine when you don't know what to do or where to turn, and when you feel as if it's all over. It could be due to a divorce, an affair, a criminal situation, or for some, the loss of something once loved and cherished.

What do you do when life takes an immediate turn? What do you do when you feel like you're about to lose your mind? What do you do when you've hit rock bottom with drug addictions, alcoholism, sexual habits, infidelity, or promiscuity? What do you do and where do you turn when your life is totally messed up?

This book is meant to encourage you and to outline a path to rediscovering your life, your dreams, and your future. I pray that as you read it, you will do as I have done: get up and live again, believing your life is not over because we serve the God of Another Chance.

CHAPTER 1
THERE IS STILL HOPE

"We must always remember that God knows how to work all things together for our benefit."

The day the Lord gave me the idea for this book, I was returning home from a weekend stay at a monastery. Fresh from my divorce, I needed to take a break to clear my mind and hear the voice of the Lord again. I needed to feel a refreshing in my spirit that I had not felt for a while. After an incredible life-changing time at the monastery, I took a long, slow drive through the beautiful countryside. The scenery was so majestic, and I sensed I needed to pull over and take a minute to enjoy the nature surrounding me.

Upon exiting my vehicle, to my astonishment, I faced one of the most picturesque open fields I had ever seen in my life. As I went closer to this heaven on earth, an overwhelming sense of God's presence surrounded me. At that moment, God began to restore me. As I stood in that open field, there were no boundaries, no distractions, and no limitations, only God and me. In that instance, I felt nothing but liberty from past guilt and shame and the unsavory choices that had plagued my life and made me feel like a failure and a huge disappointment to everyone I knew.

As I walked through the field, thanking God for my newfound freedom, it happened. I received just what I needed…to hear from God.

I had waited my entire life to hear the five words that would change me forever: "My son, I love you." Not only did these words bring me to a place of total healing and restoration, but for the first time in my life I knew what it felt like to be embraced by a father's love. Growing up fatherless, I had never experienced that fatherly love. I still desired and missed it.

As I wept in God's presence, I knew I was totally forgiven once and for all, and this was a new chance to live the life God had predestined for me.

I know what it's like when you feel as if your life is worthless or that you have committed an unpardonable sin. I know what it's like to wake up day after day wishing you could undo the hurt you have caused others. But there is hope and forgiveness in God. Romans 8:35A (KJV) asks a simple yet profound question:

> *"Who shall separate us from the love of Christ?" If we have trouble or face calamity, or if we are persecuted, hungry, destitute, in danger, or threatened with death, does it mean he no longer loves us?*

The answer is found in verse 39 (New Living Translation):

> *"No power in the sky above or in the earth below—indeed, nothing in all creation—will ever be able to separate us from the love of God that is revealed in Christ Jesus our Lord."*

My desire for you is that you will be rid of everything that has trapped you in guilt and shame and rendered you helpless and fearful of the future. You have the God-given ability to change your life and live as God has intended for you.

We must always remember that God knows how to work all things together for our benefit. So, where do you start? One of the keys I had to learn in order to move my life in a new direction was how to make better choices.

CHAPTER 2
WHY DO WE MAKE BAD CHOICES?

"Getting another chance involves learning from your mistakes and changing for the better. Your life is not over, but whatever you don't change or correct you are bound to repeat."

The Merriam-Webster dictionary defines choice as "the act of picking or deciding between two or more possibilities." Each day hundreds of choices confront us: what to eat, what to wear, which way to drive to work, and so on. All of these daily choices are parts of our daily routine, although they are not necessarily life altering.

However, there are choices that can affect the course of an individual's life—choices that involve fidelity and integrity. Far too often, people lack the ability to say no to bad choices and yes to good choices. I have counseled so many people who failed to make the right choices. At pivotal times in their lives, they said yes to things to which they obviously should have said no. They said yes to drugs, yes to mistresses, yes to lying, yes to alcohol, yes to peer pressure, and yes to poor diets and lack of exercise. In the same way that choices can have negative effects, they can have positive effects on our lives when we choose to say yes to good things such as education, fidelity, and a lifestyle that includes diet and fitness. When we learn to make proper choices, our lives are less stressful and less painful.

Where we are in life is directly connected to the choices we have made along the way. Everything we are and everything we experience can be traced back to a choice or a series of choices we have made.

Therefore, if your choices have placed you in undesirable situations, it is safe to say that proper choices can help move you in a new direction. The only difference between successful and unsuccessful people are the choices they make. We all have dreams and desires, but the question is whether you are willing to do what it takes to make your dreams and wishes come true.

THE CHOICES YOU MAKE

I CAN STILL FEEL IT! Here's what happened: When I was about ten years old, my mother asked me to see if her keys were in the car. I quickly ran out and discovered the keys hanging from the ignition. Being an adventurous boy, something clicked in my brain; I had a wonderful idea. I decided to crank up the car. My heart raced as I pushed the gas pedal of that Ford Granada and heard the engine roar. Then I did the unthinkable. I decided to shift it into drive. As an inexperienced driver, I was unaware that I needed to take my foot off the gas before doing so.

In that instant, my life flashed before my eyes. The car zoomed out of the yard and went straight into the hill directly in front of the house. Once I discovered I was still alive, I had only one thought: Momma is going to kill me! Thank God I was not hurt, and there was little damage done to the car. However, my troubles had only just begun.

Once the car was safely secured, my mother beckoned me to "the room." Whenever she spanked me, it always occurred in one particular room in the house. My sisters and I never wanted to be invited into the room, although I seemed to live there.

But that day was different, and I knew I was about to get the beating of a lifetime. My mother was furious about what I had done and proceeded to give me "the talker"—a type of spanking where she talked while she inflicted the pain. Afterward, two questions remained: how in the world had this happened to me, and how could I prevent it from happening again?

After much thought, I discovered what had led to my downfall: choices. They are the most powerful things known to humanity. Choices leave lasting impacts on our lives, and many of you are still experiencing the ramifications of yours. You can still feel the pain and effects of your decisions, as can I. What I learned that day was that I had made a bad choice.

WHY DO WE MAKE BAD CHOICES?

One of the primary reasons people make poor choices is a lack of self-value. As a pastor for more than twenty years, I have witnessed many people making bad choices simply to fit in or be accepted by a particular group.

Years ago, one of my teachers asked the class what the most powerful word in the world is. After hearing an array of responses, he solved this mystery with a shocking answer. He said the most powerful word in the world is chicken.

As a bright and inquisitive student, I could not resist the temptation. I had to ask: "Why chicken?"

His response was profound. He said, "Many people have lost their innocence, their purity, their integrity, and even their lives because someone said they were chicken."

Whenever we feel like we have to prove our worth and value, we are already in trouble. Maybe you will say, "I know who I am." Countless individuals have sat across from me and said, "Pastor, I did it because she made me feel like I still had it."

Really? Are you kidding me? We should know who we are and what rare qualities we possess.

One of the common struggles of humans, from the blossoming teenager to the seasoned man or woman, is the tendency to battle against matters of worth, value, and acceptance. People who never feel senses of worth, value, and acceptance tend to search for places where they are wanted and admired. Countless marriages have been destroyed because individuals did not feel validated by their spouses, leading them to seek acceptance and approval elsewhere.

The purpose of this statement is not to justify these behaviors but to ascertain why certain choices are made. For some reason, when people are uncertain of their value, they search for someone or something to give them validity. Have you ever wondered why a highly educated, attractive person will connect with an uneducated, unemployed person? The answer is not in the number of degrees on the wall or the amount of money in the bank. The answer lies within.

The Bible states that a man should not think more highly of himself than he ought to. The opposite is also true: a man should not have an unnecessarily low opinion of himself. Remember, your view of yourself and your self-value will be directly connected to the choices you make.

"PASTOR CHRIS, CAN YOU GIVE ME SOME ADVICE?"

This is what a business owner asked me. He had just discovered a high-profile protégé of his had gotten a young lady in the company pregnant. The protégé was a married man and a prominent figure in the company, as well as in the community at large.

My friend was confused as to how something of this magnitude could happen. I dropped everything immediately and took a flight to meet him. After I asked a series of questions, I came to one clear and concise conclusion: the young man was devoid of personal significance. This is not an attempt to blame his spouse for his behavior; no one should have so much power over you that they determine your personal value. However, when there is a loss of self-worth, people will go to extreme measures to fill the void.

I recently read a report stating that 75 percent of women in prison are there because of relationships with men who were involved in some kind of criminal activity. These women made choices based on their need to receive love and approval from people they perceived as adding value to their lives.

I can't tell you how many people sacrifice their names and reputations, their companies, their marriages, and their ministries to connect with others who have nothing to offer them. When you know your value, you ask yourself this essential question: is this person, this drug, this money, or whatever worth my losing everything? The answer is always no.

I want you to pause, take a serious look at where you are, and ask yourself, "Do I know my self-value or self-worth?"

Getting another chance involves learning from your mistakes and changing for the better. Your life is not over, but whatever you don't change or correct you are bound to repeat.

VISION

During his Pro Football Hall of Fame speech, Shannon Sharpe gave a riveting account of his childhood. He reflected on growing up poor and having to sleep in a single-bedroom house with his grandmother, brothers, and sisters. The house did not have an inside toilet and had no running water. According to Sharpe, the house had so many holes in the roof, he and his family would set up pots when it rained to attempt to catch all the incoming water.

This story would not be as surprising coming from someone who had grown up in the 1920s or 1930s. Sharpe, however, grew up in the 1980s and 1990s. He attributed his success in the NFL to one thing: his choices.

Sharpe had one thing that stayed in the forefront of his mind: he was determined to get his grandmother out of those horrific living conditions. He envisioned a day when his grandmother would no longer have to live in that house. This became the gauge by which he made his decisions.

Anytime he faced a choice or an opportunity to go astray, he would remind himself of his grandmother and her substandard living conditions. That motivation allowed him to stay focused and resist the temptation to become distracted. Sharpe established boundaries in his life to ensure nothing would prevent him from getting into college, and ultimately, the NFL.

He stated that while others were hanging out, he was working out, and while others were drinking, partying, and living the college life, he was watching football films and studying his playbook. As a result of his good choices, Sharpe went on to become one of the finest players at Savannah State College and one of the NFL's most prolific receivers.

Sharpe won three Super Bowl titles and finished his career as the NFL's leading receiver. Despite all he accomplished, the highlight of his career was the day he purchased his grandmother a new home.

How did Shannon Sharpe accomplish so much despite his obstacles? He never lost vision. The Bible says, "Where there is no vision, the people perish" (Proverbs 29:18, KJV). I want to encourage you to capture a picture of the future you desire for your children, your spouse, your parents, or yourself. The vision has to be compelling enough that you are willing to deny yourself your deepest wants and desires until it is accomplished. A good question is: what are you willing to deny yourself in order to accomplish your dreams?

VARIETY

An idle mind is the devil's workshop. This is a lesson I learned early on in life. My grandmother was an advocate of hard work, but she also believed in having fun. She would tell us funny stories, and we would laugh for hours.

Variety is the spice of life. When a person's life is destitute of variety, excitement, and fulfillment, he or she becomes more susceptible to boredom, which causes individuals to search for things that will add flavor to their lives. Boredom can greatly influence your choices causing you to compromise your standards and judgment. Many children are born to unwed mothers who were bored and fell prey to the lure of one-night stands. Countless marriages have been destroyed because of bored spouses who went looking for Mr. or Ms. Excitement. When we allow this cancerous condition to set in, we are at the mercy of the moment. I've learned that when people are bored, they are attracted to things that under normal circumstances would not stimulate their interest.

Boredom is a lack of or a hunger for excitement. This makes the condition disastrous when it's allowed to exist for extended periods.

When I hear people say, "I don't have a life," "My life is so routine," or "My marriage has lost its spark," I immediately see the warning signs. Human beings are designed to resist pain and gravitate toward pleasure. Therefore, people can remain in an unsatisfied state for only a limited amount of time. After a while, their lives will demand change, unfortunately, by any means necessary. At that point, the choice system is altered and the individual seeks fulfillment.

We make many of our poor choices when our rationale is questionable. Perhaps you are reading this book because you have gotten yourself into something that dramatically changed your life. Maybe the root cause of your problem was the inability to maintain variety in your life.

"I'M JUST HERE WORKING."

This is what a friend of mine shouted as the police raided a recording studio where he was working for a popular rap artist as a freelance graphic designer. Before that, he had been unemployed and had plenty of free time; boredom had set in, and he had decided to get out of the house and go to the studio with his rapper friend and some other artists. It seemed to be a harmless decision. What could possibly go wrong? Besides, he was tired of just sitting around the house twiddling his thumbs.

However, my friend was no novice designer or someone totally oblivious to the music industry. In fact, he had been involved in the business for more than twenty years and was well acquainted with the inappropriate behaviors that occurred in studios. Thus, his decision was a recipe for disaster.

Upon his arrival, the studio seemed safe and free of any extracurricular activities, so he proceeded to show the rap artist the changes he had made to some graphics. Right above him was a TV monitor that showed activity outside. As he glanced up, he saw police assembling and getting ready to break down the door. His heart dropped, and he immediately realized he was in the middle of a raid.

The police knocked down the door, and everyone was instructed to get on the ground. My friend quickly became aware that this was a sting operation. The police found a large amount of drugs on the premises. It became overwhelmingly clear that everyone in the studio, including my friend, was going to jail. Though he was lying on the floor with his hands cuffed, he was completely innocent and obviously a victim of circumstance. However, he was forced to suffer the same agonizing treatment as the rest of the group.

Fortunately, this story ends on a positive note. My friend was released after twenty-four hours and was cleared of all charges. Unfortunately, this story is the exception and definitely not the rule. Every day I hear about people who end up on the opposite end of the spectrum—individuals who are not as lucky as my friend and are sentenced to years in prison. The only crime these people commit is being in the wrong place at the wrong time. Many are like the biblical King David, who became bored one night and desired something to spice up his evening. He went out onto his balcony and saw a naked woman taking a bath and was moved to send for her.

David was informed that the woman was married, but he overrode his better judgment and had her brought to him anyway, totally ignoring that the man she was married to was a captain in his military. Like many of us do, he disregarded his senses and became blind to his choices. David, distracted by the woman's beauty and his boredom, became a victim of the moment; the consequences of such a decision can last a lifetime.

As you are repairing your gauges, you must choose to focus on the consequences of your decisions. When you look beyond the moment, you will be able to navigate successfully through your times of boredom because you will realize you will suffer from the drawbacks of your choices. David lost his integrity, his innocence, and even his son's life because he didn't properly handle one moment in his life.

What about you? What have you lost? What could you lose? Think about it: ten minutes of pleasure could cause you to lose ten years of your life. The question is: is it worth it? Again, the answer is no!

CHAPTER 3
THE PEOPLE IN YOUR LIFE

"I believe relationships serve as the soil or environment that allows your life to become strong, healthy, and productive."

"TAKE ME TO THE STORE."

A friend of mine was approached by one of his friends with this request, so he could pick up a few items. This seemed like a routine run, one they had done several times before. The guys had been friends for a while, but my friend was not aware that his friend had gotten into the pharmaceutical sales business—aka illegal drug dealing.

On this particular day, the dealer had a large amount of drugs in his possession. To the surprise of both men, the local authorities stopped them for a busted taillight. My friend noticed that the guy was acting peculiar and that he was stuffing something under the seat.

As the police officer advanced toward them, a heated argument was brewing inside the car. Abruptly, the dealer asked my friend to remain calm and insisted everything would be fine.

The officer asked them to step out of the vehicle. As the two of them reached the rear of the car, the officer detected my friend's nervousness and asked him the dreaded question: "Are there drugs in the car?"

My friend attempted to mask his fear and said no. However, the skilled officer saw through the smokescreen and asked if he could search the car.

I wish I could say this story has a happy ending, but life often deals out unfair hands. That day, all his hopes, dreams, and ambitions vanished right before his eyes. His friend was unwilling to claim ownership of the drugs, and both were arrested and charged with possession with the intent to distribute. Each of them received a five-year prison sentence.

How did this happen? How could someone who was trying to give a person a ride to the store end up in prison? The answer is: it happened because of the assumption of friendship. Many times people who fall from grace never become the stars they were destined to be simply because they got involved in the wrong relationship. I have heard it a thousand times: "I thought you were my friend," "I thought I could trust you," or "I can't believe you have turned on me like this." We often invite people who are nothing more than wolves disguised as sheep to hold intimate places in our lives. These relationships can completely devastate lives, reputations, and families.

This can be attributed to the misuse of the word friend. I want you to examine thoroughly anyone you have allowed into your circle. Why is this important? Because we are products of our upbringing (our parents) and our associations (our friends).

Please understand, it is not my desire to say that the people in your life control your future. Remember, you are ultimately responsible for the choices you make. However, I believe relationships serve as the soil or environment that allows your life to become strong, healthy, and productive.

There is a story in the Bible that helps clarify this argument. It is the parable of the sower, and it is found in Luke 8:11–15:

> **Now the parable is this: The seed is the word of God.**
> *Those by the way side are they that hear; then cometh the devil, and taketh away the word out of their hearts, lest they should believe and be saved.*

They on the rock are they, which, when they hear, receive the word with joy; and these have no root, which for a while believe, and in time of temptation fall away.

And that which fell among thorns are they, which, when they have heard, go forth, and are choked with cares and riches and pleasures of this life, and bring no fruit to perfection.

But that on the good ground are they, which in an honest and good heart, having heard the word, keep it, and bring forth fruit with patience.

This illustrates the power of environment. Each seed had the same promise; the difference was in the soil in which it was planted. You and I are no different from these seeds. We are born full of potential and receive the same opportunities as everyone else. However, like seeds, we have to be planted in the right environments in order to receive the nutrients, support, and love we need to flourish.

Environments shape our choices. I was having this conversation with a man who was totally convinced that environment has little influence on our choices and successes in life. After many hours of heated debate, I posed this question to him: "If you were sentenced to the toughest state penitentiary in America, how would the environment alter your current way of thinking?"

"Drastically!" he shouted—proving that environment can utterly alter someone's way of life.

Many lives have been profoundly impacted by environment, whether through decision or by deception. Some people make choices, against their better judgment, to accept, trust, or follow the wrong person or people. Others are deceived because they lack discernment and are blindly led into situations that prove unfruitful.

As you examine where you are in your life, please allow me to interject some sound advice. Take a moment and write out the names of your closest friends and family members. Once the list is complete, divide the groups into the following categories:

1. Those who add worth and value to your life.

2. Those who take away from your worth and value.

3. Those you would like to pattern yourself after in order to become a more productive person in society.

4. Those you clearly know you can't model your life, your marriage, or anything else after.

When this assessment is complete, you will need the courage to surround yourself with people who possess the qualities necessary for you to achieve the goals you have set for yourself. This is an important yet difficult part of the process. I have learned that people will make or break your recovery or rediscovery methods. To receive another chance in life, it is imperative that you evaluate your relationships. We will deal with this more throughout the book, but let's first examine the roles people play in our lives.

UNDER THE INFLUENCE

"WHAT'S THE PROBLEM, OSCAR?" This is what a young man asked a police officer who pulled him over for weaving across the lines while driving his car. The gentleman had just left a party where he'd obviously had too much to drink. Shocked by the flashing blue lights and loud siren, he rehearsed his lines to appear as poised as possible: "What's the problem, officer? What's the problem, officer?" He had said this over and over to himself, but when the officer tapped on his window with his big, black flashlight, something went horribly wrong.

Instead of asking, "What's the problem, officer?" he asked, "What's the problem, Oscar?" The officer immediately knew he was under the influence. Needless to say, the young man didn't sleep in his own bed that night.

This is a funny story, but it conveys what happens when we are under the influence—not only of alcohol or drugs, but of other people. Influence affects what we say, how we see, how we walk, and where we end up. The people who influence you contribute to the end results of your life; they structure your choices and establish the guidelines that dictate your decisions.

This often happens through observation and association. We become who we are because of what is modeled for us. One preacher said it best: "You become what you behold."

WHY AM SO I ABUSIVE?

A teary-eyed gentleman asked as he sat across from me during a counseling session. He couldn't understand why he was abusive toward his wife. He would have moments of intense anger and hostility wherein he would implode and then explode by throwing things, cursing, and even punching holes in the walls. Although he had never hit his wife, his actions left her terrified. They were meeting with me because she had reached her limit, and they were on the verge of divorce.

He said to me, "Pastor, I just don't understand it. I love my wife."

I was baffled, but I could sense he was being truthful. So, where was all this anger coming from, and was I qualified to assist them?

I have learned from many years of ministry and counseling that we discover answers by asking the right questions. After a round of intense conversation, it seemed as if I was getting nowhere. Then I asked him about his parents and the type of home in which he had grown up. This proved to be the key to the problems they were facing.

I uncovered that his father had exemplified the same type of behavior. This man was simply reenacting what had been modeled for him all his life. The behavior had been buried in the deepest parts of his being and was waiting to be released.

I was able to assist him in breaking the destructive patterns, but the majority of the work was done once he knew what was influencing him. Whether you believe it or not, your environment influences you, often without your even being aware of what's happening to you. This is why you must be careful.

When someone influences you, he or she can control and determine what your thoughts are about drugs, alcohol, sex, adultery, stealing, murder, God, church, and many other topics. Wherever you are right now speaks of the influences in your life. I pray that as you read the rest of this book, you will allow me to influence you. Why? Because I know how you feel and what you are going through. I know what it feels like to be on the bottom and afraid of what the future holds. When you have the right people in your life, they can influence you to pick yourself up and dream again. Yes, there are people who can influence you to do wrong, but there are also people who are ready to influence you to do right.

Take a look at modern celebrities who have ruined their public images. Typically, they have had the wrong types of influences in their lives. Celebrities are notorious for surrounding themselves with yes men who never challenge or correct the celebrities' bad behavior. For some reason, we are content with people who agree with everything we do. This is true even if we are doing something that will destroy us in the long run.

Think about that for a second. Do you have anyone who serves as a constant reminder that you have a lot at stake and you cannot afford to blow it? Someone who reminds you that you are married to a beautiful, loving spouse, are the father of wonderful children, or have a successful career or ministry? Most of the time, these people will surface only after total failure is achieved. My prayer is that from this point on, you will be open to the people who love you enough to confront you even when it hurts.

CHAPTER 4
THIS IS NOT A SPRINT

"I know you have experienced some kind of setback, disappointment, or breakdown, but the story doesn't end there. It's now time to begin putting your life back together."

"DOES SHE REALIZE THIS IS ONLY THE FIRST LAP?"

I can still remember the track meet like it happened yesterday. The day was sunny and beautiful yet very hot; the temperature seemed to be about one million degrees Fahrenheit. Several of the teams had some of the state's top sprinters competing. However, the distance competition was up for grabs. As a team, we had performed fairly well, but we needed the one-mile relay and mile runners to win.

The mile-relay team came in second, so we could win the meet only if our mile runner came in first. We had faith in her because we had watched her in practice, and we knew she was fast. At last, the time for the final decisive event arrived. She stepped up to the line, checked out the competition, and confidently nodded to the coach, who nodded back with the same level of confidence.

The runners came to the line, the line judge checked their positions, and the shot was fired. The race started, and our runner took off like a blaze of fire. She ran so fast, she appeared to have a trail of smoke behind her. She had an extensive lead, and all of us—her teammates—cheered her on. As she came around a corner, we noticed she turned up her speed. That was when it hit us: she didn't know this was a four-lap race. She crossed the line with her hands in the air as if the race were over. As she was informed that it was not, her countenance and body language shifted; to her surprise, she had three more laps to go. Disgust and anguish covered her face like clouds cover the sky before a drenching downpour. She had exerted all her strength and energy on one lap, not realizing there was a lot of the race left. She had given all she had in that one lap and was unable to finish the rest.

Although the young lady was an incredible runner, she had never competed in an organized track meet. She was on the team simply because someone in a physical education class told her she needed to be on the track team. The track coach had limited time to prepare her for the race, which left her totally oblivious to what was expected of her. In other words, all the parties involved had been thrown into their responsibilities without any explanations and limited preparation.

This book is a lot like that race. You have only completed one lap, but this is not a sprint. There are more laps to go. In order to help you truly get another chance, I have laid out several steps that will reposition you to get back on course. You must pace yourself and focus on getting the most out of this book. I know you have experienced some kind of setback, disappointment, or breakdown, but the story doesn't end there. It's now time to begin putting your life back together.

NOW WHAT?

In the opening pages of this book, I illustrated the depths of my fall and the agony of losing my marriage, my credibility, and nearly my mind. Allow me to repeat myself clearly: I know how it feels to hit rock bottom. But I also know how it feels to experience God's love, grace, and mercy. I can truly say that by the grace of God, I survived the worst storm of my life. How did I do it? I committed to the process of restoration. When I committed myself to God, it allowed Him to restore everything in my life. I trusted God to do what I could not.

Now I want to help you by sharing with you the steps I took. I truly believe these steps will aid your restoration. I know your situation may differ from mine, but I believe God will meet you at the place of your disappointment. If you commit to the journey, you will experience the freedom and liberty that come only from accepting the power of the one living God.

The following pages contain some simple devotionals and teachings that convey a powerful message of healing and transformation. I am not claiming these steps are an exhaustive set of methods. I only want to share with you what I did to change my life and regain my hope of a positive, successful future.

Let's take the second lap in this race. I am sure you have what it takes to finish and win strong! Get ready, because your life is about to change forever.

STEP 1
REMEMBER:
GOD LOVES YOU

"God's love is unconditional. His love will see you through any and all conditions."

"WHY CAN'T I SHAKE THIS FEELING?"

This was the question I asked myself as it became more apparent that my life was slipping completely away from me, and there was nothing I could do about it. Each day I confronted the daunting task of simply getting out of bed and facing life. I kept reaching for whatever I could to give me some sense of happiness, peace, or joy but to no avail. Depression loomed over me like a dark cloud. I couldn't shake it. I couldn't get past it. I couldn't get around it.

All I wanted to do was sleep. I was under the strange illusion that somehow I could sleep away my problems and when I woke, my life would be completely changed. To my disappointment, each morning my situation was the same as it had been the day before. I felt like a student in the university of life, constantly being given tests I knew I would fail. With each failure, my frustration increased, and thereafter, intimidation set in.

It became obvious that I was fighting an invisible opponent who was more skilled than I was and had the upper hand. My opponent never took a break; he did not need to rest. He only had one mission: to make me completely miserable. Therefore, my number one mission became finding a way to overcome this opposition.

So, I did what most twenty-first century Christians do. I turned to Google, and I began to research the symptoms of depression and anxiety. I looked at every possible answer as to how to overcome them. After researching my symptoms, I came to the conclusion that I had to get some help. Various sites recommended talking with a licensed professional. I had never visited a counselor or a psychologist in my life. I had always been on the opposite end, giving counsel. I pondered going to the psychologist as I sat at my computer. Many emotions were churning inside of me: Was I really in need of this? Could I be transparent with a complete stranger? What would people think of me after finding out I'd seen a counselor or psychologist?

This was a totally different level for me and completely out of my comfort zone. I was in a strange land. It was very difficult for me to make the initial phone call. I was nervous and sweating profusely, but as I'm writing this book, I'm extremely glad I did it. Sometimes change will occur in our lives only when we are humble enough to reach out for help, and what you will discover in the process is that you won't make it alone. It's going to take the prayers, support, and help of others to get you through this moment, especially if your moment is as difficult as mine was.

I picked up the phone and made the call. The day of my appointment came, and I found myself sitting in the office of a professional counselor. It felt like everyone's eyes were on me. Humiliation and embarrassment hit me like a ton of bricks. How had I gone from being a guy full of pride, spunk, and enthusiasm to being the guy who needed help? One of the first things you will have to confront is your pride. It will keep you from reaching for help even though you desperately need it.

That day I knew I had to face my life. In spite of how I felt, I couldn't afford to leave that counselor's office. I needed my life back again.

After waiting for nearly an hour and a half to see the doctor and watching patients come into and go out of his office, my name was called. That was when it all became a reality. It became inevitably clear that God was doing something deep inside of me. I sensed I was on the verge of a deep level of healing, change, transformation, and restoration—possibly a level I had never experienced. It was a sobering moment for me. I finally felt I was getting a grip on my life.

Face to face with the counselor, I sat there like a little child-nervous, fickle, and scared. I didn't know what to expect, but I was praying he could help me and that something good would come out of this appointment.

Then he asked me the dreaded question: "How may I help you?"

It was as if someone had turned on the sprinklers in my eyes. Without saying a single word, I began to bawl like a child. The more I tried to stop crying, the more the tears kept coming. I couldn't get anything out. I had suppressed so much for months.

Finally the tears slowed enough for me to utter, "Man, I need help." And then, "I hate myself. And I know God hates me too." I had never thought I would hear myself say these words.

The counselor was a man who understood biblical principles; he was a person of great wisdom and discernment. He quickly interrupted me. "We will deal with your hating yourself throughout the course of this counseling. First, I want to deal with your thinking that God hates you."

What he shared with me over the next thirty-five minutes was a simple teaching on the unconditional love of God. It was so profound, and it changed my life significantly.

There are three things you should always remember about the love of God:

1. **God's love is infinite.** There are no limits on His love. He loves us and is always willing to walk us through turbulent times. Above all else, the love of God says He still believes in your future. If you can remember He loves you and desires for your life to flourish, you will be able to face challenging times. His plans for us are good and not of evil—to give us hope and a great future.

2. **God's love is unconditional.** His love will see you through any and all conditions. Think about it. Most people don't plan to face problems that alter every facet of their lives. Wouldn't it be cruel for God to abandon us at the times when we need Him most? The good news is He doesn't. God avails Himself to us when we fail to live up to our full potential. Rest in the assurance that He is ready and willing to love you even through the difficult moments in your life.

3. **God's love is unearned.** It is not issued out on the basis of how well we perform. There is no measurement we are required to meet or live up to that guarantees us access. There is not one thing we can do to make God love us more, nor is there anything we can do to make Him love us any less. Our actions and attitudes may not always please God, but they never affect His desire to love and maintain fellowship with us.

Scripture

Romans 5:8 (KJV): But God commendeth his love toward us, in that, while we were yet sinners, Christ died for us.

Prayer

Father, I realize that You love me so much. I come today to receive Your love for me. I know there is nothing I can do to make You stop loving me. You are the one person who loves me regardless of how I perform. Your love is able to cover a multitude of my sins, my mistakes, and my shortcomings. I am so appreciative and grateful for Your love, which You clearly demonstrated by sending Your son to die on my behalf. Through my relationship with Christ, I can access You and all Your promises for me.

Father, I ask that You will shed Your love abroad in my heart, and I ask that I may clearly recognize how much You love and care for me each and every day. Father, I ask that You remove all feelings of self-hate and any feelings that lead me to believe that You no longer love me. I ask this in Jesus' name, amen.

Confession

Father, I declare that I am loved and accepted by You. I refuse to walk in self-hate and resist the tendency to feel that I am hated by my Father. I set my heart and mind to experience all that has been purchased for me by the death of Jesus Christ. I declare that Jesus died for me, and my sins—past, present, and future—are forgiven. I am loved, I am accepted, I am wanted, I am valued, and I refuse to allow anything to make me feel any other way.

STEP 2
REPENT AND
MAKE IT RIGHT

"To repent basically means to change for the better. There are two kinds of change: a change of mind and a change of action."

Repent! The preacher shouted the first time I went to church. It was as if someone had pulled out a gun and started shooting in the place. There was such fear and reverence that covered the room. I wondered why this one word had brought such conviction. Later, I asked a friend of mine what repent meant, and once I heard his definition, I discovered why. Far too often in the church, repentance is connected to negative connotations. For many, repentance is in direct correlation with someone going to hell. In many Christian circles, repentance has become one of those terms like hell, Holy Ghost, or speaking in tongues—you just don't say it. Why has this word that is used numerous times throughout scripture become taboo?

In the twenty-first century church, I believe, a growing number of believers have thrown the baby out with the bathwater. Many think repent or repentance is a negative word, but actually it is one of the most gracious words in all of the English language. To repent simply means to change your mind and go in a different direction. Just think: if you lack the ability to change the course of your decision, you will also lack the ability to deter negative consequences in your life. This is what makes repentance a beautiful thing: it makes it possible for us to change our minds and directions when we recognize that our attitudes and actions will produce undesirable sets of consequences.

To repent basically means to change for the better. Let's examine this change further. There are two kinds of change: a change of mind and a change of action.

1. A change of mind

   a. About sin: "I have disobeyed you, Lord."
   b. About self: "I can't do this alone."
   c. About our attitudes and mindsets: "My thoughts are not His thoughts."
   d. About a course of action: "I have taken a wrong turn and gotten off course."
   e. About Christ: "I must allow Christ to express Himself through me."

2. A change of actions

   a. I will allow Christ to express His character through my life.
   b. I will change my mind, my attitude, my opinions, and my beliefs.
   c. I will change my will, my decisions, and my determination.
   d. I will change my emotions, my godly sorrow, my remorse, and my regret.

Repentance is a word that suggests several things:

1. Wisdom. When we repent, we operate in sound judgment by demonstrating a respect for God and His word. When we fail to repent, we indirectly and directly state a disposition of pride. We directly offend God by suggesting we are above His judgment. Wise men and women are not above error or sin but will recognize that they have missed the mark and quickly return to God. The word of God makes it clear that pride causes individuals to fall and be humbled.

Proverbs 29:23 (KJV): A man's pride shall bring him low: but honour shall uphold the humble in spirit.

When we are wise, we humble ourselves and activate the mercy of God in our lives by repenting of our wrong.

2. A relationship with God. There is a difference between individuals who attend a church and those who have vibrant, life-giving relationships with God.

Repentance is a relational word that indicates we have wronged someone. Out of our love for God and other people, we repent and choose to walk away from anything that offends. Repentant is the most sincere we can become and proclaims that we take responsibility for our actions.

When we repent, we state to God that the deepest part of our being longs to be in right relationship with Him. Therefore, we refuse to allow lust, jealousy, lying, gossip, or any such thing to hinder our relationship with Him. Repentance says to God, "I can't go on knowing I have wronged You and violated our relationship."

In the book of Psalms, David stated, *"Against you, you only, have I sinned (Psalm 51:4A NIV)."* David had wronged others, but he had sinned against God and hurt their relationship. Repentance is not only wanting to change from the sin; it is grieving over the fact that you have sinned.

2 Corinthians 7:10 (KJV): For godly sorrow worketh repentance to salvation not to be repented of: but the sorrow of the world worketh death.

Paul told the church at Corinth that there are two kinds of sorrow. One is godly sorrow, which leads us to change our lives for the better. Then, there are the sorrows of this world, which cause us to grieve when we lose things in this life. As Christians, we should never have more sorrow when we lose things than when we jeopardize our relationship with Christ.

3. **Gratitude.** Thank God we have an advocate with the Father, so when we sin, we can repent and ask for forgiveness. The apostle Paul made it clear that we should not use this as a license to sin. Isn't it awesome how God provides a means for us to change our minds for the better and go in a different direction?

4. **A clean break.** Repentance is not an on-again, off-again type of thing. Repentance is the act of totally breaking free or doing a 180. Repentance is the resolve that I will never do this again, and I trust in my relationship with Christ to keep me free of this sinful activity in my life. Although repentance is an ongoing part of our Christian experience, we should reach a place where certain things are out of our lives for good. The mere fact that I am repenting clearly states that I have found something in my heart that contradicts the word of God.

The Bible is filled with individuals who had to repent: Moses, Noah, and even God Himself. As you apply these steps, God will meet you with the grace you need to overcome the weaknesses in your life. But in order for you to get the most out of this time, we must start with repentance.

The following exercises will help you to walk through the process of repentance. I recommend you do one exercise per day.

Exercise 1

Repent for Generational Sin

Find a quiet place and ask the Holy Spirit to reveal to you any sins, attitudes, or patterns that have flourished throughout your family, and *write them on a blank sheet of paper.* It is best to do this exercise early in the morning while everyone is asleep and with no music. As the Holy Spirit speaks, write down what He says.

> **Nehemiah 1:4-11 (KJV):**
> *And it came to pass, when I heard these words, that I sat down and wept, and mourned certain days, and fasted, and prayed before the God of heaven, And said, I beseech thee, O Lord God of heaven, the great and terrible God, that keepeth covenant and mercy for them that love him and observe his commandments: Let thine ear now be attentive, and thine eyes open, that thou mayest hear the prayer of thy servant, which I pray before thee now, day and night, for the children of Israel thy servants, and confess the sins of the children of Israel, which we have sinned against thee: both I and my father's house have sinned. We have dealt very corruptly against thee, and have not kept the commandments, nor the statutes, nor the judgments, which thou commandedst thy servant Moses.*
>
> *Remember, I beseech thee, the word that thou commandedst thy servant Moses, saying, If ye transgress, I will scatter you abroad among the nations: But if ye turn unto me, and keep my commandments, and do them; though there were of you cast out unto the uttermost part of the heaven, yet will I gather them from thence, and will bring them unto the place that I have chosen to set my name there. Now these are thy servants and thy people, whom thou hast redeemed by thy great power, and by thy strong hand.*
>
> *O Lord, I beseech thee, let now thine ear be attentive to the prayer of thy servant, and to the prayer of thy servants, who*

desire to fear thy name: and prosper, I pray thee, thy servant this day, and grant him mercy in the sight of this man. For I was the king's cupbearer.

1. Say this simple prayer: Holy Spirit, there are some things broken in my life and in my family. I ask that You reveal the sins of my forefathers that are attempting to act out in my generation.

2. Get quiet and write down what you hear. Example: the Holy Spirit might reveal rebellion or pride, lying or stealing, divorce or adultery, poverty or sickness.

3. Whatever you hear, regardless of how simple or silly it might be, write it down. This could be the key to your life turning around. Pause and listen some more to make sure the Holy Spirit has finished speaking.

4. Repent for every sin you see on the page. Sample Prayer:

    Father, in the name of Jesus, I repent for my family and myself for the sin of rebellion that runs through my bloodline. I declare that this sin will not have dominion over my bloodline or me. I renounce this sin of rebellion in Jesus' name. I am free of rebellion, and I follow the voice of Jesus only. Amen.

    (Do this for each one you write down)

5. Rip up the paper and declare your freedom in every area.

6. Remind God of your covenant rights:

Father, I declare that Jesus became a curse for me, and therefore, no curse has a right to remain active in my life! I am free from all curses.

7. Shout for victory and praise God for Jesus Christ, your Lord and Savior.

Exercise 2

Repent for Personal Sin

Find a quiet place and ask the Holy Spirit to reveal to you any sins, attitudes, or patterns that have flourished throughout your family, and *write them on a blank sheet of paper.* It is best to do this exercise early in the morning while everyone is asleep and with no music. As the Holy Spirit speaks, write down what He says.

> **Psalm 51:1–8 (NKJV):**
> *Have mercy upon me, O God, According to Your lovingkindness; According to the multitude of Your tender mercies, Blot out my transgressions. Wash me thoroughly from my iniquity, And cleanse me from my sin. For I acknowledge my transgressions, And my sin is always before me. Against You, You only, have I sinned, And done this evil in Your sight—That You may be found just when You speak, And blameless when You judge. Behold, I was brought forth in iniquity, And in sin my mother conceived me. Behold, You desire truth in the inward parts, And in the hidden part You will make me to know wisdom. Purge me with hyssop, and I shall be clean; Wash me, and I shall be whiter than snow. Make me hear joy and gladness, That the bones You have broken may rejoice.*

1. Say this simple prayer: Holy Spirit, I ask in Jesus' name that You reveal to me anything present in my life that does not bring glory to Your name.

2. Get quiet and write down what you hear. Example: the Holy Spirit might reveal rebellion or pride, lying or stealing, divorce or adultery, poverty or sickness.

3. Whatever you hear, regardless of how simple or silly it might be, write it down. This could be the key to your life turning

around. Pause and listen some more to make sure the Holy Spirit has finished speaking.

4. Repent for every sin you see on the page. Sample Prayer:

> *Father, in the name of Jesus, I repent for the sin of _____. I declare that this sin will not have dominion over me. I renounce this sin of _____ in Jesus' name. I am free of _____, and I follow the voice of Jesus only. Amen.*

(Do this for each one you write down)

5. Rip up the paper and declare your freedom in every area.

6. Remind God of your covenant rights:

Father, I declare that Jesus became a curse for me, and therefore, no curse has a right to remain active in my life! I am free from all curses.

7. Shout for victory and praise God for Jesus Christ, your Lord and Savior.

Exercise 3

Repent for Relational Sin

If you are married, this is a wonderful exercise for you and your spouse to do together. Find a quiet place, and ask the Holy Spirit to reveal to you any sins, attitudes, or patterns that are present in your marriage or other relationships. It is best to do this exercise early in the morning while everyone is asleep and with no music. As the Holy Spirit speaks, write down what He says.

Matthew 6:14–15 (KJV):
For if ye forgive men their trespasses, your heavenly Father will also forgive you:

But if ye forgive not men their trespasses, neither will your Father forgive your trespasses.

Ephesians 4:26 (KJV):
Be ye angry, and sin not: let not the sun go down upon your wrath:

1. Say this simple prayer: *Holy Spirit, I ask in Jesus' name that You reveal to me anything present in our marriage (or relationship) that does not bring glory to Your name. Also reveal to me anyone I have not forgiven or anyone I am having a hard time forgiving.*

2. Get quiet and write down what you hear.

3. Pause and listen some more to make sure the Holy Spirit has finished speaking.

4. Repent together (if married) for anything that has gotten into your marriage. Also, forgive any person that has offended you.

Sample Prayer:

Father, in the name of Jesus, I forgive _____ of any and all offenses, and I refuse to hold this against [him or her] any longer. I declare that from this moment, I will no longer allow anything to hinder my relationship with _____. I am free to love and respect _____ regardless of how [he or she] has treated me in the past.

For Couples:

Father, in the name of Jesus, we recognize that _____ has gotten into our marriage, but we refuse to allow _____ to destroy our marriage. Therefore, we take authority over the devil and declare that we have victory over _____ in our marriage in Jesus' name. Amen.

Move on to the next one.

5. Rip up the paper and declare your freedom in every area.

6. Remind God of your covenant rights:

Father, I declare that Jesus has made me free, and whom Jesus sets free is free indeed.

7. Shout for victory, and praise God for Jesus Christ, your Lord and Savior.

Make It Right with Your Brother

James 2:8 (KJV):
If ye fulfil the royal law according to the scripture, Thou shalt love thy neighbour as thyself, ye do well:

Matthew 18:15 (KJV):
Moreover if thy brother shall trespass against thee, go and tell him his fault between thee and him alone: if he shall hear thee, thou hast gained thy brother.

Matthew 5:24 (KJV):
Leave there thy gift before the altar, and go thy way; first be reconciled to thy brother, and then come and offer thy gift.

Years ago, I dealt with issues of unforgiveness, and I went through the whole process of saying to God that I forgave a person who had hurt me. But for some reason, feelings of resentment and hostility toward this individual remained. During a time of prayer and fasting, the Lord revealed to me that I had not properly handled this area of my life. The Lord instructed me to get the situation right between myself and the individual.

I replied, "Lord, what else can I do? I have released him to You."

His response was, "You must go to him and correct the relationship."

That was a defining moment in my life because this particular individual had betrayed me in a major way. However, I understood that my blessings would be held up until I got this situation corrected. What the Lord was saying to me was I had to make it right with my brother.

Many of you are trying to figure out why certain things in your life are not flowing the way they should. There's a possibility that you have not handled an issue of unforgiveness correctly. You must understand the difference between making it right with God and making it right with your brother. We do only half of the process and expect a whole return. I have spent hours trying to convince people of the importance of going to their brothers or sisters and making it right, often to no avail. Any time you are hurt, disappointed, or discouraged by an individual, you are offended. An offense left unattended grows into something much larger and much worse.

Anytime you develop negative feelings toward a certain person, you are required to make it right. Which means you must go and ask him or her to forgive you in order to get all animosity out of your heart. Also, you must reestablish proper channels with God. Who is that person who has offended you, but now God is requiring you to go to him or her and repent?

Exercise 4

1. Say this simple prayer:

   Father, I discovered that a certain relationship in my life is suffering due to my unforgiveness. This is difficult for me because I feel there is no need for me to go to this person and ask for forgiveness. But out of obedience to You, I willfully obey and trust Your word. Father, I ask that You bring peace into this situation. Today it is my desire to speak to _____ and close all doors of unforgiveness. I ask You to heal every wound that has occurred to my family and me and _____ and [his or her] family. Today I will have victory over the devil as I allow the character of Christ to flow in my life.

2. Contact the person, share the offense, and reestablish the relationship.

3. Say this simple prayer:

   Father, in the name of Jesus, I have done as Your word requires, and I thank You for the joy of obedience. I ask that You guard my heart against offenses and unforgiveness, and as You have forgiven me, I pray I will forgive others in Jesus' name, amen.

STEP 3
RECEIVE GOD'S FORGIVENESS

"Where you have been is only a fraction in comparison to where you can go."

"I DON'T REMEMBER WHAT YOU ARE TALKING ABOUT!"

This is what I said to a gentleman who was trying to explain to me how he had hurt and offended me some years back, and now he wanted to ask for my forgiveness. He was persistent in his attempt to refresh my memory. Almost an hour into the conversation, it finally dawned on me what he was talking about, and I also understood why it had been hard for me to remember this particular offense: I had not been as impacted as much as he had thought. I told him all was well, and I had forgiven him, but he continued to reiterate how sorry he was for speaking against me and my ministry.

Again, I said, "Sir, I forgive you." It wasn't sinking in. He began a third time apologizing and going over the details of the story. Then I realized: this guy does not understand what it means to be forgiven.

I could no longer stand the redundancy. Trying to sound as sincere as I could, I said, "Sir, you don't get it. I forgive you."

He quickly responded, "But you don't understand."

I replied, "But I do. Although you were wrong, I forgive you, and I do not hold your actions against you."

With much amazement, he looked at me and said, "Thank you."

Far too often, we fail to realize that our heavenly Father is so willing to forgive us. We complicate forgiveness and make it a long, drawn-out process. What does it mean to forgive? It is to pardon or release from a debt. What the gentleman in this story didn't understand was that I was releasing him from the debt, and he didn't owe me anything at all. We often struggle with this concept because we are constantly trying to pay for our sins. God's love for us is so strong. He is more willing to forgive us than to punish us for our sins. We are so accustomed to working hard at gaining the approval of others, we can't comprehend this level of forgiveness.

More often than not, people will make it hard for you to receive forgiveness by convincing you that God is more into your destruction than your deliverance. God's goal is to bring you back to a place of oneness with Him and to restore you. Friend, God is more committed to your future than to your past, and He has great plans for you, but you must receive His forgiveness. Look at it from a natural standpoint: What parent would want to destroy his or her own child?

Why do we struggle with receiving forgiveness? It can be summed up with one word: guilt. This is a human attempt to pay a debt that can be satisfied only by forgiveness. Until we understand the power of forgiveness, we will waste time and energy attempting to obtain a sense of emotional and internal peace. True peace with God and self is possible only through giving and receiving forgiveness.

Today, if you turn to God, He will completely forgive you for your sins and failures. Through God's, forgiveness you can discover a new hope that leads to a positive and powerful turnaround in your life. In step two, I took you through the complete process of repentance, which addresses actions, but forgiveness addresses attitude. When we walk in forgiveness, we appreciate the grace and mercy afforded to us by the shed blood of Christ, through which we have been forgiven. This forgiveness is not earned or purchased but is simply something we must receive.

Today you can be liberated from the pains, failures, and disappointments of your past by saying a short confession: *Father,*

I receive Your forgiveness, and I adjust my attitude to agree with the mercy You have made available to me.

This statement repositions you to be successful in receiving God's forgiveness, which allows you truly to forgive yourself. When you have successfully forgiven yourself, your future will look promising. It allows you to embrace the first day of the rest of your life. Allow me to help you position yourself to receive forgiveness.

FIRST, STOP BEATING YOURSELF UP.

One aspect of the human experience is disappointment, and we will have all have our fair share. Throughout the journey of life, you will be disappointed and you will disappoint. Often, it is not our intention to hurt, but it can occur due to conditions beyond our control. However, there are times when we are well aware that our choices and actions will upset and disturb the lives of others. Needless to say, we can find ourselves drawn to dangerous and destructive patterns like a moth drawn to a flame. We become enamored with the beauty of the flame but fail to see the danger of getting too close. Here is where we make choices that change the course of everything we are connected to.

Many who lack the skills to handle the pressures of worldly temptations will often lack the ability to accept the consequences that come about in the process. We have a natural tendency to feel ashamed and guilty whenever we face negative circumstances, whether we are the victim or the victimizer. This overwhelming guilt can cause an overcompensation as we try to repay ourselves for the damage we have caused. Receiving God's forgiveness requires that you forgive yourself. As long as there is a deep feeling of unworthiness, the process to receive forgiveness is prolonged.

You cannot receive forgiveness from God or man as long as your perception of yourself remains out of alignment.

Here is the deal: no amount of self-inflicted pain and punishment will change what has to happen to you or by you. And to be totally honest, the weakest and most unfruitful place for you to release your energy and efforts is in your past. The past should serve as a teacher, but if you are not careful, it will serve as a guard that will keep you locked in. Some of you, if you are like me, have never spent a day in jail but have spent years as a prisoner of your past.

It reminds me of one day when I was walking through the mall in Atlanta and all of sudden I heard, "Chris Evans!" This call came from an old acquaintance from my college days. We reminisced about the good old days—the parties, the drinking, and even some things I had forgotten. As the conversation progressed, I began to search for the opportunity to tell this lady that I was no longer the guy she had once known. But I could not get a word in. She went on and on about the fun we used to have in the past, and then she asked if we could go out and do the town. This was my opportunity, and I knew I had to seize it.

I looked at her and said, "What I'm about to tell you is going to shock you."

She immediately went to the extreme and said, "Don't tell me you're gay."

I smiled and said, "Heavens no. I am a preacher of the gospel."

She laughed.

I said, "No, I'm serious. I'm a preacher."

"You?" she said.

I replied, "Yes, me."

"How did this come about?"

I gave her my testimony of how the Lord saved me and changed my life completely.

"So, you don't live like the old Chris I once knew," she said.

I replied, "No. I am a changed man."

"I don't believe it," she said. "No one can change to that degree."

She was determined to get me to party with her one last time. But I continued to share how Jesus Christ had come into my heart and radically changed my life. I could see the amazement and embarrassment on her face as the reality of my conversion set in. She looked at me and said, "So, you've really changed."

"Yes," I said. "I am a different man."

"Wow. I can't believe it," she said. "You were so bad."

What was the problem here? She was stuck in the past and could not believe that Jesus Christ had drastically changed my life. Maybe this is your problem. It is extremely difficult to move into your future while holding on to your past. You must find a way to let go of yesterday. As difficult as it is to believe, you are not the same person you were before God completely changed you. You must walk into your future. I cannot encourage you enough to believe that your future is bigger than your past was.

SECOND, START LOOKING AT YOUR FUTURE.

Recently I taught a message at my church about the difference between the rearview mirror and the windshield. You cannot afford to live your life looking through your rearview mirror, through which you can see only what is behind you. The windshield is wider and allows you to see much farther. The rearview mirror represents your past, and the windshield represents your future and the endless possibilities you can possess.

In scripture, God promised Israel a land they had never seen, and He brought them out of Egypt into the Promised Land. From this moment on, I want you to look for your "Promised Land." Your life is not over, but you must stop looking in your rearview mirror and start looking through your windshield. There is so much left for you to accomplish, but you are the only person who can take hold of your future and make it a reality. Receiving God's forgiveness is about letting go of the past and laying hold on your future.

Receiving God's forgiveness is about releasing and receiving. To release means to remove anything that confines or stops progress. The goal of this book is to get you to release your past, which, if you allow it, can stop you from moving forward. What a tragedy it would be to stop at this point in your life without discovering what your future holds. My friend, I promise you that your life is not over, and God will get some glory out of what you are currently facing. But in order to see what will come out of this moment in your life, you must continue moving forward. Stopping now would mean your current situation is the final chapter in your book, and I believe you are a winner. Therefore, you must press into the next phase of your life, because I promise you, it is better than you think.

Scripture

1 John 2:12 (KJV): I write unto you, little children, because your sins are forgiven you for his name's sake.

Prayer

Father, Your word declares that I am forgiven. I thank You that You no longer see my sins or shortcomings; You see the precious blood of Jesus. I ask You to help me be conscious of Your forgiveness. I ask that You remove any guilt or shame. I want to be free of my past failures, and I believe that the blood of Jesus makes it possible for me to have total and complete healing and restoration. I ask this in Jesus' name, amen.

Confession

Father, I declare that I am forgiven. When You look at me, You see only my future, not my past. I declare that I am freed from the penalty of sin. I am no longer under the Law but under grace. I declare that Your grace is sufficient for me, and I declare that it empowers me to live a complete and victorious life. I declare that I am free from all mental and emotional torment as a result of my sin. Your forgiveness releases me to press forward with my life, and I declare that I will seize every opportunity to live a full and satisfying life. Father, You have not discounted or disqualified me, and I choose to not do it to myself. I choose to see myself as You see me.

STEP 4
REDEDICATE YOUR LIFE

"Whenever I sense that I am losing my edge, without hesitation, I go through a time of rededication."

"YOU DID WHAT?"

This is the reaction I get when I tell people about my past struggles. It's amazing that most people see you where are but fail to realize where you have been. Maybe you are in a different time in your life or in the process of rebounding from a difficult season. Regardless of where you are, praise God for your journey.

As we move through the first phase of this book, I want you to look back over the last few days, months, or years of your life. What series of events stick out in your mind? Most people's memories serve as initiators of both joy and pain, and we feel most of our joy right after we succeed over our greatest pain. What do you do when things go wrong and you fall into some type of sin, or someone you love fails horribly in his or her morals? Perhaps you are not confronting a moral failure, but something has zapped your fervor and strength for God and His will for your life. How do you come back when life deals you an unexpected blow that leaves you numb and lifeless?

Each week I have the responsibility of preaching to my congregation, and each message is normally lined with something to remind people to praise and worship God. One day while driving home, I asked the Lord, "Why do you want me to tell people to praise you when they should want to praise you anyway?" I later discovered that people are so bogged down with the cares and concerns of life, they forget the source of all life. God is the answer, but many believers appear to need more convincing. Sometimes we need a refreshing or renewal in the spirit. Sometimes we all need to rededicate our lives to Christ.

LORD, I REDEDICATE MY LIFE

There are moments when you feel so close to God, and things work like clockwork. We are focused and clear about our lives and futures and are excited about our relationship with Christ. I remember years ago a young man joined my church who was such a radical person for Christ. He would dance and shout without shame or reservation. I remember hearing some of the members saying things like, "He's on fire now, but give him a couple weeks, and he will calm down." I laughed and agreed with them because I had been like that young man once. But through time and routine, I lost that fire and passion to praise God with all my strength and might.

What happened? Did God stop being God? No! Did he stop providing for me and blessing my life? Of course not! As a matter of fact, I have more material possessions, money, influence, education, and spiritual knowledge now than I've ever had. So, what happened?

I see this pattern in the lives of so many believers who lose their zeal and passion for Christ. They don't shout, dance, or have that radical edge anymore, and some don't even realize it. Where did it go, and how can a person get it back?

Whenever I sense that I am losing my edge, without hesitation, I go through a time of rededication. Why? Whenever I sense that my fire for Christ and His work is leaving, I must find out what is stealing my attention. Remember, friend, you have a personal relationship with Christ, which is just like any other relationship: it must be maintained. For example, a man does not just lose his desire for his wife. Somewhere there has been a violation in the relationship.

Human beings are designed in such a way that they can't give their full attention to everything at once. Even multitasking has its limits. Therefore, we must find those things that have caused breaches in our relationship with Christ and have caused us to become more dedicated to other things than to Him. Anytime we go through a time of repentance, we should follow that with a time of rededication.

WHAT IS REDEDICATION?

In order to understand what it means to rededicate, we must understand what it means to dedicate. The word dedicate means several things:

- To set apart for a deity or sacred purpose; to consecrate.

- To devote oneself to something fully, wholly, and earnestly.

- To set aside for or assign to a specific function, task, or purpose.

When something is dedicated, it is reserved strictly for one person or thing. Everyone is dedicated to something: doctors are dedicated to medicine, lawyers are dedicated to the law, pastors are dedicated to the Bible, students are dedicated to school, and Christians are supremely dedicated to Christ.

When we are dedicated to God, we are reserved strictly for His purpose and His use. The scripture states, "Ye are bought with a price: therefore glorify God in your body, and in your spirit, which are God's" (1 Corinthians 6:20, KJV). When a man marries a woman, he is dedicating himself to her and indicating that his focus is strictly on meeting her needs and covering her life. These same principles govern our relationship with Christ. We have declared our allegiance to Him and His purposes. However, there are times when a Christian can drift away from this commitment and pursue other things and even other gods. We can break our dedication by allowing other things to become our focus.

There have been times when my agenda has elevated itself over God's plan for my life. There are times when Christians yield to sinful actions or attitudes they know directly contradict the God to which they have dedicated their lives. In my twenty-plus years of ministry, I have watched many dedicated Christians go off the scene, never to resurface. When we lose our dedication to Christ and His church, something else has captivated our attention, thereby leading us astray and away from Him.

When this happens, repentance and rededication are necessary. Rededication is a new dedication. When we rededicate our lives, we are declaring a new dedication to God. We are simply stating that we are returning our faith and focus of our relationships to Him. I believe that whether we have fallen into some gross sin or not, we should consistently rededicate our lives to Christ. Each day we should declare a fresh commitment to Him and refuse to give attention to anything else. Whenever we engage in a time of repentance, we should rededicate our lives to Him and shift our attention away from the things that lure us away from Him.

Scripture

1 Timothy 4:15 (KJV): Meditate upon these things; give thyself wholly to them; that thy profiting may appear to all.

Prayer

Father, I fully surrender myself to Your will and Your word. Father, make me aware of anything and everything that has been released to cause a distraction in my life. My desire is to remain on course with the plan and destiny You have for me. Holy Spirit, You are my guide and keeper, so I yield to Your leading and Your direction. Help me hear Your voice, and Your voice only, during this critical stage of my restoration process. Father, I ask that you position me to be an instrument in Your hands and allow my story, my struggles, and my triumph to be blessings to someone else. I ask this in the name of Jesus.

Confession

Father, I declare a new dedication to You and Your will for my life. I return to my purpose, and I declare that I will complete every assignment. I receive and rely upon the person and the power of the Holy Spirit to lead, guide, and direct me. I declare that where He leads, I will follow. I am confident that I hear His voice, and I will obey every command. I will not walk in the fear of failure. I will resist every thought that suggests I will not uphold this commitment. I will trust in the Lord and in the power of His might to uphold me with His mighty right hand. I declare that I am victorious in every aspect of my life.

STEP 5
REMOVE ALL RESIDUE

"When you recap your past pleasures or pains, you reactivate feelings and emotions that allow you to relive events of the past."

"WHAT DOES IT TASTE LIKE?"

That was the question I asked my guest who said his drink tasted funny. What happened? In my haste to prepare for my guests, I had forgotten to rinse the glasses thoroughly after washing them. Instead of my guests tasting soda, the beverage was overpowered by soap.

Sometimes we can't understand why things seem funny in our lives, or why we can't get focused regardless of how hard we try. Could it be that there is residue from things in your life that have not been entirely removed?

What is residue? Residue is a small amount of particle that is left behind after the main particle is gone. Even though residue is small, it can drastically impact whatever it is attached to. Whenever impressionable moments occur in our lives, residue remains. We find fingerprints or impressions of the person, decision, or pain left behind just as they are left at a crime scene. This residue can shape our views of the future or limit our ability to move forward. I have known countless individuals who found themselves stuck because of what was left behind. Others are overly paranoid and lack the ability to trust themselves or others because of residue. These small or microscopic substances have brought many lives to a complete standstill.

Why is residue so powerful? Because, as it did with the glass, it affects the senses. Residue, if not removed, can impact how an individual sees, feels, or hears. Residue can also serve as a seed that produces a future harvest. When residue is allowed to stay, it hinders our ability to experience life from a healthy perspective. Residue, although small, doesn't remain in that state but can grow to dominate and stir all human choices.

Have you ever wondered why people move from bad relationship to bad relationship or bad choice to bad choice? The answer is simple: RESIDUE. They attempt to move forward without getting it all out.

HOW IS RESIDUE REMOVED?
1. **You must make a decision.**

Years ago, a lady called me and said she was struggling with trying to get over her ex-boyfriend, whom she had broken things off with months earlier. Through a series of questions and simply listening, I discovered she still had pictures of him in her house; love letters he had written and gifts he had given her were tucked away in a keepsake box. On her cell phone were all the messages he had texted her, and to top things off, she was still wearing the engagement ring he had given her! When I asked her why she was holding on to these things, her response was, "I'm believing God will help this relationship work itself out. So I wanted to hold on to the items."

Immediately, I saw that she still had soap in the glass and had not truly made a decision to break away from this man. This woman was literally fooling herself. She thought she could hold on to everything that reminded her of him, yet escape the grip of this relationship. She soon discovered this was impossible.

For some of you, it's not physical things you are holding on to, but it's the memories. These memories are facilitating your inability to let go and move on. When you recap your past pleasures or pains, you reactivate feelings and emotions that allow you to relive events of the past. I want you to decide to let them go. Let them go regardless of how good or bad they were. If you really want to move on, you must be willing to remove the residue in its entirety. Perhaps you want to experience a new level in your relationships with Christ, but lurking in your present are unresolved issues from your past. How can you successfully go on with your life if you are more determined to hold on to your past than to reach for your future? Maybe your spouse hurt you, or your child has disappointed you a time or two. In order for the relationship to flourish, you must be willing to remove the residue. You can't meet your Mr. Right if you are holding on to Mr. Wrong. I have counseled so many people who say they were done with a person or a situation, but then I discovered something totally different.

2. **You must have courage.**

When clearing away unwanted residue, please keep in mind this might not be the easiest thing to do. This process may require a great level of courage. Courage is the ability to go forward even when we are afraid or uncertain. Letting go of something we deem valuable can be challenging. When we have been hurt by someone, to give up our right to retaliate or be revengeful can test the strongest among us. When something is so wrong but it feels so right, it can generate reluctance in us. Many of you have erected things in your life, whether good or bad, that must be torn down. Sometimes, as we must make the decision to move forward for the better, we discover that many decisions we make will not be popular with others. People or habits that are not good for us can grip our lives with an unbreakable hold. As I will discuss later in this book, I have encountered many who lacked the courage to put proper distance between them and something that was not good for them.

I want you to experience the freedom and breakthrough that is only possible through cutting all ties, regardless of who or what it offends.

There was a king in the Bible named Hezekiah who walked in this level of courage. Israel, as a nation, had taken a road God never intended and was suffering as a result of their choices. When King Hezekiah took the throne, his first order of business was to remove the residue of his predecessor.

King Hezekiah destroyed all the idols in the temple in the beginning of his reign as king of Israel. Above all, he removed all residue and staked his claim to follow the will of God. By learning how to remove the residue, you will position yourself to overcome bad memories, wrong motives, past mistakes, and negative mindsets. When this process is complete, you will go to a new level in your relationship with Christ.

Whether you have forgotten or have chosen not to deal with certain things in your past, now is the time to reexamine everything that has left an imprint on your heart. When the soap is completely removed from your glass, the taste will change dramatically!

Scripture

2 Kings 18:4A,6 (KJV): He removed the high places, and brake the images, and cut down the groves, and brake in pieces the brasen serpent that Moses made. For he clave to the Lord, and departed not from following him, but kept his commandment, which the Lord commanded Moses.

Prayer

Father, I pray that You would give me courage to cut all ties with my past lovers, failures, attitudes, hurts, and disappointments. I pray that You will redirect my attention and strength. Fulfill Your will and Your plan in my life. Father, some things are hard for me to let go of, but today I choose to clean house so I can receive all You have for me.

Confession

Father, I declare that from this moment on, I will be like Hezekiah and remove everything from my life that I know does not please You. Father, I will remove these things from my life and my presence. I declare that I have the courage and power to stand through this time of transition and will completely fulfill Your will. Father, I praise You in advance for the provision You will make, and I ask You to replace everything I have lost with Your perfect will for my life.

STEP 6
REESTABLISH FOUNDATIONAL PRINCIPLES

"Sometimes in life we face leaning tower experiences where everything under us seems incapable of handling the loads of our lives."

Building a strong life, family, or business is a lot like building a house. Everything rests on the quality of the foundation and framework. This step is crucial in the process. We live in a time of reality shows, because the bulk of Americans enjoy looking into the lives of successful people. Most are attracted to the glitz and glamour of the super wealthy or super successful. From mega yachts to mega mansions, we receive a glimpse into the life we wish we could have. However, this attraction can be misleading without an understanding of the price of success. Many are fascinated with what is produced but have never captured the essence of the process. True success is produced only by proper principles. Not having the right principles is equivalent to building a house on a shaky or faulty foundation. Externally, the house may be glamorous, but the true character of the house is revealed in the presence of a storm. Storms expose shortcuts or oversights in the building development.

Certain elements are unseen and unmentioned but are necessary for a firm structure. There are some corners you don't want to cut because it will cost you later. I learned a valuable lesson about foundations while touring Europe.

"THAT TOWER IS LEANING."

This is what I said on a trip to Italy. I visited the famous Leaning Tower of Pisa where I learned the importance of a proper foundation.

The Leaning Tower of Pisa was constructed over 177 years in three phases. In 1173, after a time of military success and prosperity, the people of Pisa decided to build a bell tower. The tower was intended to stand about 180 feet high. The first floor was constructed of solid marble with pillars. In 1178, construction was started on the third floor, and an amazing discovery was made: the tower was beginning to lean because of a soft spot in the foundation. It was not strong enough to support the massive structure. The builders had poured only a three-meter foundation and had not prepared the soil properly to handle the load of the building, causing it to sink.

Isn't it amazing that this discovery was not made until the builders were well into the construction of the tower? This is how our lives are: we often build on unstable principles or foundations that work at one stage or phase of our lives, but not at others.

How is your foundation? How do you reestablish an unstable foundation that cannot support what you are trying to build? Do you tear it down and start the project over? For almost a century, the people of Pisa halted the construction of the tower; doing so allowed the soil under the foundation to settle. To ensure the tower didn't completely fall over, they added stabilizers to hold it in place.

Sometimes in life we face leaning-tower experiences where everything under us seems incapable of handling the loads of our lives. We must learn from the Pisans and allow things to settle down, then continue to build. Sometimes we need a stabilizer or something to cover our miscalculations or mistakes. That stabilizer is the Holy Spirit.

The apostle Paul stated, "When I am weak, He is strong." That's how it is in our lives: you don't have to destroy everything you have built over the years; simply allow the Father to reestablish your foundation so you can continue to build your dream. Today the Leaning Tower of Pisa is one of the most admired structures in the world. Tourists come from all over just to gaze at this phenomenon because they cannot believe it is still standing. Likewise, people will come to see you because you decided not to give up on building your dream. My friend, allow the Holy Spirit to stabilize your life and dreams, and watch things turn in your favor.

ANOTHER KEY COMPONENT IS THE FRAMEWORK

This is a lesson I learned while building my personal home.

"Where did all the wood go?"

That was the question I asked the contractor who was building my house. I had ordered more than enough two-by-fours, two-by-sixes, and two-by-eights. But when I arrived on the job site, all the wood was gone. My first assumption was that someone had stolen it. The contractor explained that I had ordered enough wood, but I had forgotten to consider bracing and support.

I quickly replied, "Why do we need so much bracing and support?"

He helped me understand that the bracing supported the framework, which secured the structure of the house. He had to make sure that in the event of a storm, the house would be well-equipped with the proper reinforcement to handle it. Then I clearly understood why the house needed the bracing.

When we are taking steps to build a solid relationship with the Father, we must make sure we have put in enough bracing to ensure we can weather the storms of life.

What does it mean to reinforce? Reinforce is actually a military word. When the military is trying to take a particular territory, there are times when they must send in reinforcements. To reinforce means to provide additional strength, effort, or personnel.

When we have failed in certain areas of our lives, we need to reinforce those areas. As you are rededicating your life, you must discover what broke your dedication and where reinforcement is necessary.

There was a family in my hometown that was known for fighting; if you fought one, you had to fight them all. Because this legacy was so widespread, an individual thought twice before picking a fight with any member of this family. That's how it should be in your life: the devil should think twice before attacking your marriage, your finances, or your mind because you have reinforcements. The more people you have who can come to your aide, to pray with you or give you sound counsel, the better. Far too often we are lone-ranger saints trying to fight problems alone. Yet the Bible states that in the presence of many counselors, there is safety. We must learn the value of relationships and accountability.

Who do you have in your life as reinforcement? Who can you call when you are tempted or struggling or just need someone to talk to? If you are wise, you will make sure your spiritual house has proper reinforcement.

Scripture

Luke 11:5 (KJV): And he said unto them, Which of you shall have a friend, and shall go unto him at midnight, and say unto him, Friend, lend me three loaves.

Prayer

Father, I pray in Jesus' name that You will surround me with the people I need to reinforce my life. Father, it is my desire to walk out every aspect of my assignment and fulfill everything You have called me to do. Therefore, I ask that You help me by sending the right people into my life that I may complete my mission here on earth, in Jesus' name I pray. Amen.

Confession

I declare that I have all the relationships and accountability I need to continue to walk through this moment in my life. I declare that I will stand regardless of the turbulence, storms, or tests I may face. I have faced enough, and I am assured that I can handle whatever comes my way. Jesus, You are my strength and my refuge.

WHAT DO I DO NEXT?

One of my favorite movies is The Shawshank Redemption. In this movie, a man named Andy Dufresne is sentenced to prison for a crime he didn't commit. During his sentence at Shawshank Prison, he meets a gentleman named Red. Andy and Red become best friends. Andy tells Red if he is ever released from prison, he will go to a particular location in Texas, and he says if Red is released, he should venture there as well and find something Andy would hide for him. After a series of circumstances, Andy is pushed beyond his limits and decides to break out of prison. When he's gone, Red grieves as if he has lost a loved one. One day he receives an unmarked postcard, and he knows that Andy has reached his destination.

Years pass, and Red, who has served forty years in prison, comes up for parole and is released. He gains the courage to go to Texas. He finds the spot of which Andy spoke. After digging in dirt and rocks, he pulls out a little tin box that contains a couple thousand dollars and a note. In it, Andy tells Red, "If you are reading this, that means you have made it to this place."

Allow me to welcome you to this point. I pray that, like Red, you have been released from some things that have held you. Maybe you were not in a physical prison but an emotional one that has limited your ability to function. Regardless, you have made it to this point, and I pray there has been some kind of release. You have started moving your life in a brand-new direction, and this is only the beginning.

In Andy's letter to Red, he also says: "If you've come this far, maybe you're willing to come a little further." This is a challenge to

Red because it requires him to break his parole, which restricts him from traveling beyond certain boundaries. Andy is encouraging Red to break all the barriers and experience real freedom. I am not encouraging you to break the law but to cast off all limitations and pursue all God is calling you to do.

To reap the benefits of this book, you will need to go further. Up to this point, we have been reflective in our approach. We have looked at how things occur in your life. I have given instructions to get you on track. Now we must shift to a restorative approach. I want to show you how I restored my life and gained the courage to press past my pain and regain a sense of purpose.

Next I will outline several critical steps that will aid you in recovering what you have lost. These steps are vital to your success. I urge you to go further!

STEP 7
REFOCUS YOUR LIFE

"A broken focus is the first step in the direction of failure."

"WHAT IS THIS SUPPOSED TO BE?"

That's what you would ask if you saw some of my cousin's pictures. Have you ever known someone who was passionate about photography, but when he developed his shots no one could understand what was in the pictures? My cousin loved to take pictures at every family event, and she would take pictures of everything. The problem was, when the pictures were developed, they were all cloudy and blurred. We all would wait to see them and would be disappointed every time because they never came out right. She became legendary for taking bad pictures; eventually no one expected her pictures to come out correctly.

The problem was she never learned how to focus her camera to take the best picture. She could see the image she wanted to capture but could not adjust her lens properly. Many people are like my cousin: they have never gained the ability to focus their lives to fulfill their destinies. I have counseled countless individuals who have lost their way and can't seem to get back on course.

Why is focus so hard to get and keep? This problem can be summed up in one word: distractions! Life is full of them. Perhaps you are reading this book because some distraction has taken you down an undesired path. Maybe materialism, greed, or some other indulgence has captivated your attention, luring you into the forbidden. Isn't it amazing how long it takes to build something and how quickly it can be taken away? A business, a house, a car, or even a family is gone because someone got distracted. Once we are distracted, our lenses are out of focus, and regardless of how hard we try, we can't capture life's images with clarity. A broken focus is the first step in the direction of failure.

The devil doesn't care what he uses to break your focus as long as your focus gets broken. The Bible is filled with individuals who started strong, but their focus broke, leading to the derailment of their destinies.

Adam was distracted by his wife. The person given to be his helper, friend, and life partner got distracted, and she broke his focus. God had strictly commanded them not to eat of the tree of the knowledge of good and evil, but through satanic enticement, she yielded and encouraged her husband to do so as well. Adam was distracted by a person, and as a result of his choices, both he and Eve lost their places in the garden.

Do you know someone who was given a position or responsibility that connected him to the wrong person, and the consequences were devastating? Possibly in your life you have aligned with the wrong person or group, and you see the results of their influence. Take a minute and evaluate the people in your life. Are they aiding your focus or your distraction?

King David was distracted by his passions or appetites. A beautiful woman named Bathsheba was taking a bath, and David saw her and sent for her, knowing she was married to a man in his army. David had sexual intercourse with her; she became pregnant, and he had her husband killed to cover up his sin. From that moment on, King David's life was stained by this distasteful act. What caused him to override his common sense and complicate his life to this degree? David could not say no to his appetites. What about you? Has your inability to control a passion, a habit, or an addiction caused your life to go off course?

Samson was distracted by his pain. He had an incredible calling and a promising future but allowed the pain of his heart to distort his view and abort his destiny. Samson was married to the love of his life, but his wife was taken from him and given to his brother. This scattered Samson's emotions and drove him into the arms of Delilah, who persuaded him to share the secret of his strength. Out of a need to identify with someone he perceived as caring for him, he revealed his secret. Delilah cut his hair, and his strength was gone; Samson became like any other man.

Samson forfeited his future because of the unresolved pain in his heart. Why do we do what we do? What causes talented individuals to nullify their promising futures and chase mirages? What pain from your past is obstructing your view of the future God has intended for you?

If distraction is the greatest enemy of focus, then distortion has to be the greatest enemy of results.

"Don't take that picture." That's what I said to my cousin while attending a family reunion.

She said, "Why? This is the picture I want."

I said, "Maybe, but it will not be the picture you are going to get."

"Why?" she asked.

"Because your lens is out of focus, and the image will be blurred and distorted," I replied. I then set her camera on autofocus, and she never took another bad picture.

Merriam-Webster dictionary defines distort as "changing something so that it is no longer true or accurate." Life's trials have a way of reshaping images and causing them to be something they are not.

"I am not your ex-wife."

This is what a young lady I counseled shouted at her fiancé. Here's the story. They were in the middle of their premarital counseling, and we hit a bump in the road. She came into the session completely perplexed and frustrated and couldn't understand why she had to answer every time she was a few minutes late or if she wanted to have some alone time or a night out with her girlfriends. Each time these things occurred, she noticed his attitude toward her would change. She would be hit with tons of questions as if she were being interrogated for murder. I could see the pain in her eyes and stress in her face as she pleaded for clarity, especially seeing she had never been unfaithful or lied to him in the course of their relationship.

After many examples and much anguish, we got to the root of the problem, which was his previous relationship. His previous marriage had ended in an affair between his best friend and his wife. This incident left him scarred, guarded, and relationally distorted. In other words, he now looked at every woman through the lens of his ex-wife. But here is the kicker, he had no clue of what was happening. He assumed he was just cautious.

ARE YOU BEING CAUTIOUS OR ARE YOUR LENSES DISTORTED?

Past pains and problems can have both positive and adverse effects. They aid us in the remainder of our journey. We can learn from the mistakes we've made and from the mistakes of others. When we take this approach, pain strengthens our decisions making us wiser because now we are more equipped to make better choices.

We are more qualified to choose after much patience, prayer, and observation. Some hurts we don't ever want again. To ensure this, we maturely approach life, relationships, business, and purpose with experience. However, there is the negative.

Pain can distort how you see things, and we know perspective is everything. You cannot allow the last season of your life to summarize the rest of your life. When we go through hard moments such as bad relationships, poor choices, and missed opportunities, we sometimes park in those moments. This gentleman had parked. He had decided that every woman was like his ex-wife, and he was going to take the necessary steps to make sure he controlled the outcome of his future relationships.

If you want to make the most of this time with God, you must refocus. Your lens is how you look at life, and if it is out of focus, every image you capture will be wrong somehow. Therefore, do not allow pain, people, or passion to prevent your forward progress. Refocus your lens and gain a clear view of your destiny.

Scripture

Colossians 3:2 (KJV): Set your affection on things above, not on things on the earth.

Prayer

Father, in the name of Jesus, I ask You to help me to set my focus. I realize this world is full of distractions and temptations, so I ask You to help me stay focused on my assignment. I pray, Holy Spirit, for a heightened sensitivity to Your voice and Your direction. I pray You adjust my focus so I may see life as You see it. I ask You to change how I see my life and my future. I ask this in Jesus' name, amen.

Declaration

Father, I declare that today is a focused day, and I see only Your plans for my life and my day. I declare that You will lead me to clarity for my life, my family, my finances, and my destiny. I declare that I hold power over every distraction and temptation of the enemy. I declare that I have a healthy, positive, optimistic view of my day and my future. I declare this in Jesus' name, amen.

STEP 8
RESPECT BOUNDARIES

"If you want to finish well and make the most of the rest of your life, you must establish boundaries."

"HALT! WHAT ARE YOU DOING HERE?"

This is what an officer from the Department of Homeland Security shouted at me at a private airport in Oklahoma City. I was attending graduate school at the time, and one of my classmates had invited me to see his plane. I had a fascination with planes, and I was like a kid in a candy store. There were so many hangars. I felt like we looked at every plane on the lot, but I hadn't seen a Gulfstream, and it was my dream to own one someday. Right when I was about to give up hope of seeing one up close and personal, we walked up to this hangar that had two beautiful jets inside. As we approached, we saw surveillance cameras and signs stating, *"No Trespassing"* and *"All Trespassers Will Be Prosecuted."* I looked at my friend, and our curiosity got the best of us. We decided to go in and take a look.

We discovered that these were not ordinary planes. They looked super high tech, like spy planes. Simultaneously, we came to the conclusion that we needed to exit this hangar quickly. Just then, someone said, "Stop where you are and step away from the plane!"

As we turned, we saw two officers with guns drawn, and I thought I was going to have a heart attack. I said, "Are we in trouble?"

"Yes. You guys are trespassing on government property," one of them said.

"Government property?" I asked.

"This hangar belongs to the Department of Homeland Security."

Well, after much questioning, they discovered we were not terrorists and decided to let us go. The officers informed us we could have gotten into some serious trouble and possibly been shot for trespassing.

How did two innocent spectators get into so much trouble? We simply overstepped our boundaries. The warning signs had explicitly told us not to proceed, and we chose to disrespect that. Most of the trouble we face in life can be traced back to some boundary we ignored or broke. In a car accident, someone didn't stay within the boundaries that govern driving. The physical ailments that plague our lives are due to our ignoring the boundaries that govern good health. Marriages fail because someone didn't respect the boundaries that govern marriage. Wars break out because a nation refuses to respect another nation's boundaries. What boundaries have you ignored or failed to establish?

If you want to finish well and make the most of the rest of your life, you must establish boundaries. What is permissible or not permissible in your life? In your family? Your career? The same goes for dating, finances, employment, friendships, habits, eating, and so on. Boundaries say "this can happen" or "this cannot happen" in a particular area of your life. Once you define your boundaries, you have total authority, and when there are trespassers, you can say, like the Department of Homeland Security, "Stop! You have no right to be here."

Take a moment and look at the critical areas of your life to see where you need to establish boundaries.

BOUNDARIES OF ENERGY

"Was he the greatest fighter ever?" Someone asked me this question as I walked into a barbershop discussion. I am an avid boxing fan, so this was right up my alley. I quickly jumped in to give my opinion of who was the greatest fighter of all time. Of course, only one name could come out of my mouth: Muhammad Ali. He was a boxing genius because he knew how to transform with every phase of his career. He went from being an electrifying, lightning-fast boxer to the inventor of the famous rope-a-dope, a boxing technique designed to allow fighters to punch and punch until they ran out of energy. This technique gained notoriety in Ali-Frazier III when Ali used it to wear out the slugger from Philadelphia and defeated him in fourteen rounds.

This style of fighting was also put to the test against the invincible George Foreman, a serious power puncher. Fight analysts questioned if Ali's rope-a-dope could withstand this level of punishment. Ali baited Foreman to perfection and forced him to waste needed energy. The fifth round visibly fatigued Foreman, and Ali knocked him out in the eighth. The boxing world was shocked: how had the impossible happened? Foreman had failed to manage his energy properly; he had wasted it on useless punches and was not able to finish strong.

This is the goal of your enemy: to drive your life in such a way that you waste your energy and effort on useless or meaningless tasks. But today, you will stop wasting your energy and time on things that bring no lasting rewards.

One of the most disappointing things in life is coming to the end of your days and realizing you wasted your talents, gifts, and abilities. So many people are deceived by the illusions of this world. There was a man in the Bible who used all his energy and time to accumulate wealth. Once he had a comfortable amount, he decided to eat, drink, and be merry. "But God said unto him, Thou fool, this night thy soul shall be required of thee: then whose shall those things be, which thou hast provided?" (Luke 12:20, KJV). One of the main lessons we learn is to use our energy correctly to build things that are lasting and meaningful.

Where have you invested your energy? In your children, your marriage, your future, your God? There are 168 hours in a week. Start redirecting to invest energy on things that will cause you to win the fight of life. Come on, you can do it!

VALUES ARE BOUNDARIES

"You are always on the phone!"

This is what my son said to me as we were driving to dinner. I did not realize I spent so much time on the phone. Generally, I returned all calls while driving in my car, but I did not realize I was totally neglecting my son. I was indirectly communicating to him that he was not as important as the people I was speaking with on the phone.

Sometimes, if you are not careful, you can miscommunicate your value system. I love my son, and there is nothing more important to me than my children. But that day, I wasn't communicating to him how important he was to me. He felt I wasn't paying him any attention or that I didn't value our time together. What messages are you sending to the people in your life? Sometimes we show them they are not important to us by how we spend our time and resources. We demonstrate that we do not value them. What is your value system?

One key to gaining a second chance is reassessing values. When we lose sight of our values, we lose the navigational system of our lives. In other words, your value system guides your life, and without it you are like a ship without a sail. My son was expressing to me that he didn't feel like he was a part of my value system.

When we go through difficult times, this is one of the first things that is challenged. Is my value system that important? If you are going to recover from any fall, failure, or setback, you must rediscover what you value. I have ministered to countless individuals who lost hope in marriage, love, friendship, and God, all because things had gone wrong in their lives. Just because an area of your life fails doesn't mean you should give up on that area altogether.

Value suggests importance. What is important to you? As you are releasing the past, you must reestablish your values. Pain has a funny way of robbing you of them and leaving you wondering what matters to you. I want to encourage you not to allow your pain to redefine your values. I know so many people who say they will never, ever allow themselves to get in that predicament again. What are they stating? That they will no longer value what they used to. But whatever was of value before should still be of value to you now. Life goes on! Do not allow your past or your pain to reshape your values. If you actually want a second chance, you must reestablish your core values.

TIME BOUNDARIES

"That clock is wrong!" That's what the coach yelled at the referees calling the game. We were playing in an old gym. The game was tight, and it was obvious it would come down to the final shot. So, the coach called a time-out and strategized his play. There were ten seconds left in the game, and we ran the play to perfection. As we counted down—ten, nine, eight—the point guard released the ball, and it went in. The team shouted in jubilation.

But there was a problem: the buzzer did not sound. After much argument, we discovered the bulbs in the clock had blown, and there had not been ten seconds left but eighteen. So there were eight more seconds left in regulation.

Even though this was an equipment malfunction, the opposing team was given the ball. They drove the length of the court and scored a basket with one second left on the clock. We lost the game, not because they beat us, but because we had thought the game was over, and it wasn't. We'd thought we were dealing with ten seconds when actually there were eighteen seconds on the clock.

Has the devil tried to change the time in your life? Has he attempted to make you believe that your game is almost over? Many of you are drawing up plays of desperation under the assumption that you are running out of time. The Bible declares in Daniel 7:25A (KJV): "And he shall speak great words against the most High, and shall wear out the saints of the most High, and think to change times and laws." The devil wants to amend the time in your life. He wants to make you believe that your time has run out—that the game of your life is over. Do me a favor: take your fingers and place them on your neck. Do you feel a pulse? If you do, you are not dead and your time is not over. Yes, you have missed it; yes, you have gotten off course; yes, something has set you back or possibly knocked you down. However, if you have a pulse, you are still alive.

Why don't you say it out loud? "I am not dead yet." This means you have more time and more work to do. Therefore, do not spend this time stuck in your past. Dedicate the rest of your time to your future. Do not waste another day looking at the wrong clock with the wrong time. You have more time left to accomplish every mission

God has for you. It is imperative that you release your past and do not waste another day reliving or replaying it. Friend, it is over. Let it go. Your best days are still to come!

Scripture

Ecclesiastes 10:8 (KJV): He that diggeth a pit shall fall into it; and whoso breaketh an hedge, a serpent shall bite him.

Prayer

Father, in the name of Jesus, I ask You to forgive me for overlooking boundaries. I clearly recognize that You have placed them in my life to keep and protect me from my tendency to be tempted. I know You love me, and I refuse to see boundaries as punishments but as safeguards to assist me. Father, You know me better than I know myself, and I ask You to help me place full confidence in the love You have for me. I ask You to forgive me for any damage my behavior has caused and that You restore those I might have affected. I ask this in Jesus' name, amen.

Declaration

Father, I declare that today I surrender to Your guidance and Your leadership. I will follow where You lead. I will do what You say, the way You say it. I put my trust in You, and I will not attempt to manage my life outside Your boundaries. I declare that I will manage my life, my family, my finances, my health, and my future according to Your boundaries. I declare this in Jesus' name, amen.

STEP 9
REFUSE TO REPEAT YOUR MISTAKE

"Today I want you to accept what has happened but also accept that your life is not over. Put it behind you and move on, and God will give you the strength you need to succeed."

"NOW, THAT WAS STUPID!"

I know we should never call anyone stupid, but sometimes the things we do make absolutely no sense.

Here's the story: I once knew a guy who had committed a crime when he was a young man and had been sentenced to twenty years in prison. After serving his time, he was released and given another chance to exist in society. After a couple months of freedom, this gentleman committed the same crime he had committed more than twenty years earlier. When he went before the judge, he was sentenced to another twenty years in prison.

Why do we repeat the same stupid mistakes that cause us to lose precious time in our lives? It seems like we would learn the first time around. As ridiculous as this may sound, it is a common thing in the lives of so many people. Throughout my ministry, I have counseled many people who were habitual violators, repeating the same things over and over again. From giving people who severely hurt them more chances to making bad financial choices, having multiple children out of wedlock, and going back to drugs and alcohol, we often do things that are unprofitable.

Today is a significant step in the process of your turnaround because you are going to make a calculated decision to walk away from the hang-ups in your life. What is a calculated decision? Every day we make tons of decisions. Decisions range in difficulty and consequences. Not only do decisions vary in effect, but we arrive at conclusions through different means.

Common decisions are the ones we make without much thought. Brushing your teeth or driving to work are common decisions we make every day, and we often do them while doing other things at the same time.

Then there is the coerced decision. We arrive at this type of decision by someone or something forcing us to decide. In other words, this is not the course of action we would choose, but due to unique circumstances, we are compelled to come to a particular conclusion.

When I was in elementary school, I decided to join the band. For some crazy reason, I decided to play the trombone. I don't think I really knew what the trombone was, nor that my mom expected me to bring it home every day. Keep in mind I walked about two miles to my school, so this was quite a feat to lug a heavy trombone case every day. I decided to leave it at school and make my trip to and from school easier. This did not sit well with my mother. After a couple of warnings, she decided to inflict some pain to reinforce her recommendation. At this point, I was introduced to my first coerced decision. From that day forward, I made sure I carried that instrument home.

Coerced decisions are effective as long as the external stimuli is present. Coerced decisions are often not long lasting because the decision to change was external. The decision was initiated by someone or something else. For the most part, individuals lack a clear understanding why the decision is necessary. Typically, the moment the external stimulus is removed, a regression to the previous behavior occurs.

The best type of decision we can make is a calculated decision. In a calculated decision, we gain the ability to decide, even when the gratification is delayed. When we make a calculated decision, we are able to factor in the pain or difficulty of the decision we are about to make. Unlike coerced decisions, we arrive at calculated decisions based on a decision from within. Others may support your decision or even influence your decision, but at this point you realize why you need to do this.

I can't promise you that your decision will be easy or without resistance. You can decide to never repeat certain behaviors, release certain people, and recover from certain circumstances.

"It's not that easy!" you say. Well, I agree with you. This is possibly the most difficult decision you will ever have to make. But I promise, it will also be the most rewarding.

It's never easy to walk away from someone you care about or something that has a grip on you, but it is possible. There is one thing you must do in order to start this process: you must make that decision. Until you decide that you will not live in this predicament, you are bound to remain in it and eventually repeat it. I believe if you are reading this book, your desire to better your life is evident. With that in mind, be willing to pay the price to produce results you can live with.

But what happens if you fail in your attempt to move forward? First, let me say life is full of setbacks. You may experience some as you try to break free. The key is knowing how to handle them when they occur. How do you handle it when your attempts to progress are unsuccessful? Or you find yourself falling into the same predicament over and over again? You simply forgive yourself.

Forgiveness is the common thread woven throughout this book. When we forgive a person or ourselves, we simply eliminate a debt.

Forgiving yourself says, "I let myself off the hook, and I will get up and try again." Forgiving yourself postures you to defeat your two greatest enemies: guilt and regret.

GUILT AND REGRET

"I can't believe I fell into this again." This is what a young man said as he sat in my office sobbing. He had fallen grossly into sin. He had an alcohol addiction that he had triumphed over for several years. For some reason, this terrible addiction was gripping his life again, rendering him helpless and defeated. What a sad story to have victory in your life over a particular habit or situation, and all of a sudden that thing regains control.

What do you say? How do you handle the devastation of losing to an old enemy? I encouraged this young man to get over his mistake; regardless of how long he had been free, he could be free again. Immediately I noticed that his greatest enemy would not be the alcohol, but the regret—the voice of loss or failure that forces us to assess damage based on how much time or effort has gone into developing certain areas of our lives. The greater the amount of time or effort that has gone into it, the greater the level of regret or grief we feel.

Regardless of how much I talked about forgiveness and the mercy of God, he only reflected on how much time he had spent away from this substance. Maybe your situation is different. Maybe you've invested time and effort into a marriage, children, a business, your sexual purity, or friendship, only to be utterly disappointed. The most common responses to this type of failure are regret, guilt, and disappointment. But whether the guilt or disappointment is in yourself or in someone else, you must move on and away from this pain. You should not be nonchalant about it; the feeling is necessary to ensure that you never revisit this place again. However, it should not be permanent.

I have met countless people who live in guilt and regret. The marriage has been over for years, but one spouse is still living with the regret. The house or car has been repossessed, but the regret lingers. I have been there so many times, and I know you kick yourself because you know it is partially your fault; we play parts in everything that happens in our lives. Maybe you disagree with me, but you must accept that while you might not have played a major role in what caused the pain, you are totally responsible for how you dealt with it.

Today I want you to accept what has happened but also accept that your life is not over. Put it behind you and move on, and God will give you the strength you need to succeed.

HOW DO I DO IT?

First, realize it is a process. There is no way you are going to experience this level of disappointment without some pain. You are not abnormal for feeling what you feel, my friend. You are normal. It's normal to feel down, hurt, and even like giving up. You are not superhuman, just a human being with real feelings and real emotions. With that in mind, know that some things take time to overcome.

Second, you need a plan. How will you move forward with your life? Remember, you might not have contributed to getting where you are, but you are the only person who can plan to get you out of this place. As difficult as it may seem, I encourage you to write out your plan to move on with your life.

Third, it will require praise. Yes, that's right: give God praise for where you are and for where you are going. Your life will not always look like it looks right now, and you are entitled to another chance.

Psalm 42:11 (KJV)

Why art thou cast down, O my soul? and why art thou disquieted within me? hope thou in God: for I shall yet praise him, who is the health of my countenance, and my God.

Let's say it together: "I refuse to repeat." This is your daily confession. Anytime you are tempted, stop and say, "I refuse to repeat." Sometimes we complicate things, but it's that simple to control your destiny.

Realize where your help comes from. Once you decide never to repeat, the Holy Spirit can supply the power you need to support the decision you have made. Notice the order: once you make the decision, the Holy Spirit can make it possible. Say it again, "I refuse to repeat."

Scripture

2 Corinthians 12:9 (KJV): And he said unto me, My grace is sufficient for thee: for my strength is made perfect in weakness. Most gladly therefore will I rather glory in my infirmities, that the power of Christ may rest upon me.

Prayer

Father, in the name of Jesus, I come and ask You to give me the strength to remove things from my life that are no longer working or effective. Only You know my future, and I ask You to replace these things with the tools, people, principles, and resources I need to succeed. I ask for wisdom and guidance to help me as I move forward with my life. I turn to You, Father, to reveal anything that needs adjusting in my life. I ask that the Holy Spirit lead me on the path of righteousness. I know He will lead me to Your perfect plan and perfect will for my life. I ask this in Jesus' name, amen.

Declaration

Father, I make room for You to release a new strategy in my life. I declare that I will break free of all things that prohibit my growth and advancement to my purpose. I praise Your name for freedom and complete deliverance from anything that is unnecessary or inadequate for my future. Take them away from me, as far as the east is from the west, and never allow them to return. I declare that today I will walk in the newness of life and adjust my attitude and heart to walk away from anything You no longer want me to have. I declare this in Jesus' name, amen.

STEP 10
REWRITE YOUR STORY

"You can allow life to write your story, or you can take out your pen and rewrite it."

> *And it came to pass, that when Jehudi had read three or four leaves, he cut it with the penknife, and cast it into the fire that was on the hearth, until all the roll was consumed in the fire that was on the hearth.*
>
> *Then took Jeremiah another roll, and gave it to Baruch the scribe, the son of Neriah; who wrote therein from the mouth of Jeremiah all the words of the book which Jehoiakim king of Judah had burned in the fire: and there were added besides unto them many like words.*
>
> —Jeremiah 36:23, 32 (KJV)

Jeremiah, a prophet in the Bible, wrote a letter to King Jehudi, but the king cut it up and threw it in the fire. When the prophet heard this news, rather than getting discouraged, he took out his pen and rewrote the letter, adding to it as well.

Wow . . . what a story. Maybe this connects with where you are right now. Maybe you wrote out plans for your life, and it seems as if they have been ripped up and thrown into the fire. Or possibly you feel your life should be further along than it is, but for some reason you can't get where you want to be. Why has discouragement set in? Why have you lost your hope for the future of which you've always dreamed? Well, possibly you have allowed something to interrupt what you perceived to be your promising future. In life, you must always plan for the unexpected problems you think will happen to someone else, not you. But for some reason, they knock at your door, and now what do you do?

NOT MAGIC

One of the difficult but memorable events in the history of sports was the Earvin "Magic" Johnson press conference in November of 1991. The suspense was incredible as rumors circulated in regard to

Magic's future in the NBA. I can remember news reports circulating and attempting to clarify what Magic was going to say. And then it happened. Magic took the podium and shocked the world by announcing he had contracted the HIV/AIDS virus. No one saw this coming. Magic was revered and loved by so many. Every kid on basketball courts across the world emulated and imitated his game. He was a part of the big three: Michael, Magic, and Bird.

Could it possibly be the end of one of professional basketball's greatest eras? Magic had an impressive resume and was one of professional sports most celebrated stars. Known for his million-dollar smile and incredible finesse, Magic's announcement was difficult for many because it seemed to happen to such a rare talent and an outstanding person. One question loomed after his announcement: What's next for Magic?

How do you recover when your whole world is stripped away from you? What would he do or how would he survive seeing this threat to his livelihood? What a sad state for anyone to be in, especially someone so beloved. Well, whatever happened to Magic Johnson? Did he have a nervous breakdown? Did he lose everything he had worked to acquire through his illustrious career? Did he go into hiding from the shame and guilt of his past choices? Was basketball his only gift and talent? Absolutely not! Since his jaw-dropping announcement, Magic has piled up accolades, achievements, and wealth.

He won a gold medal with the 1992 "Dream Team." He is the CEO of the Magic Johnson Enterprises, a billion-dollar conglomerate which includes "ASPiRE," a television network; Magic Johnson Bridgescape academies, which help high school dropouts get diplomas; and Clear Health Alliance, which helps provide healthcare for HIV/AIDS patients. He once owned 105 Starbucks and 4.5% of the LA Lakers, which he later sold for $100 million. He bought ownership in the Los Angeles Dodgers for $2.15 billion, which is the most money paid for a North American sports franchise. He is worth $500 million, with Magic Johnson Enterprises worth $1 billion, making him one of the most successful black men in America. How did he do it? Magic Johnson realized that he could rewrite the story. He refused to let that chapter be the end of the book.

I have ministered to so many people who never thought they would go through what they are currently facing. A divorce, a rape or molestation, an abortion, an addiction—what do you do when such problems visit you? You can allow life to write your story, or you can take out your pen and rewrite it. I recommend the latter. Life is a series of decisions, and one you must make is to overcome your past failures by rewriting the story of your life. Maybe you are not happy with the chapters up to this point. Well, why not sit down and write the conclusion of your life? How do you want it to end? With you being a success and on top of your game? If that is what you want, put the past in the past and rewrite the final chapters of your life this way.

Abraham Lincoln was a complete failure for the first forty-plus years of his life, but he decided that the remainder of his life would be different.

FACTS ABOUT LINCOLN:

1832	Lost job and defeated in state legislature
1833	Failed in business
1835	Sweetheart died
1836	Suffered a nervous breakdown
1838	Defeated for speaker
1843	Defeated for nomination for congress
1849	Rejected as land officer
1854	Defeated for US Senate
1856	Defeated for vice presidential nomination
1858	Again defeated for US Senate
1860	ELECTED PRESIDENT

Lincoln learned to never give up and kept rewriting the chapters. Even though his life ended tragically, Lincoln went down, not as a failure, but as one of the greatest presidents in the history of the United States of America.

Today, I want you to glean from these examples, and know if they did it, you can too.

Take out your pen and start rewriting.

Scripture

Jeremiah 36:23, 32 (KJV): And it came to pass, that when Jehudi had read three or four leaves, he cut it with the penknife, and cast it into the fire that was on the hearth, until all the roll was consumed in the fire that was on the hearth. Then took Jeremiah another roll, and gave it to Baruch the scribe, the son of Neriah; who wrote therein from the mouth of Jeremiah all the words of the book which Jehoiakim king of Judah had burned in the fire: and there were added besides unto them many like words.

Prayer

Father, I realize my life is not over regardless of what has happened to me up to this point. I understand that You are in control of everything, and I choose to believe that the best is yet to come. Today, I take my pen and rewrite the chapters of my life, and I ask You to help me to know that how things are is not how they will be. Change is coming for me, and I ask You to reveal Your plan for my life. I thank You in advance for working on my behalf. I am excited about my future. I ask this in Jesus' name, amen.

Declaration

Father, today is the first day of the rest of my life, and I decide to rewrite my future. From this moment on, my life will be destiny focused. Therefore, I declare success and prosperity over my life, and I declare that failure is no longer going to dominate my life. I declare this in Jesus' name, amen.

STEP 11
REALIGN WITH
YOUR PURPOSE

"Get up and realize your worth and your value."

"THIS CAR DOES NOT NEED TIRES."

This was my argument with the service tech at Mercedes-Benz. I took my car in for a routine checkup and was met with some expensive news. The gentleman gave me the results of his inspection of my vehicle—everything was normal, but he concluded by stating, "Oh, by the way, you need some new tires."

He gave me an outrageous price for the tires—something in the neighborhood of $475 each. Once he picked me up off the floor, I argued that the tires on the car still had good treads.

"They do, Mr. Evans," he replied. "But look on the insides of the tires."

As I looked more closely, I discovered that the insides of the tires were completely worn. I didn't understand how they could have good treads on certain parts and be completely bald on others.

My service tech explained that a Mercedes-Benz needs an expander to align the car and prevent improper tire wear. Of course, this expander was not free; in fact, it was rather costly. I questioned my tech to see if the problem could be solved for a cheaper price, but he insisted this was the only way. He further explained that until I had this service done, I would continue to wear out my tires and this could cause a tire to blow out. After much debate, I decided to put in the expander to align my car properly and prevent this problem from reoccurring.

Our lives are often similar to my Mercedes-Benz. We, too, get out of alignment. What's wearing thin in your life? Is it your health? Your marriage or family? Your finances? Your relationship with God? Your purpose? Alignment is critical to success in life. As we come to the close of this book, I want you to realign with the will of God for your life.

The busyness of this world can get you out of balance, causing you to wear thin in various areas and lose sight of what is important or meaningful. So many people are unaware of their alignment issues and end up wrecking their lives without ever knowing the problem. Alignment issues can go unnoticed until something fatal occurs. The average person struggles daily with alignment but struggles even more with getting things back into their proper places. Over the last couple of years, my life was completely out of alignment.

A better term for alignment is balance. When we are balanced, we are focused and living in accordance with our purpose in life. How do things get out of alignment or balance? This was the question I posed to my service tech. And his response is applicable to this part of the book. He said, "Potholes in the road. The deeper the hole, the greater the damage."

Many of you have hit potholes, or the various struggles, situations, and adversities you have encountered. Some were small and manageable, but others were deep and life altering. Take a minute and list out some of your potholes. Also, write out what effects these experiences had on you.

The road of life has potholes that can drastically affect our alignment and cause us to get out of balance. I have met several people who never recovered from their potholes. They no longer talk about the rest of the road left to travel, because they are constantly reminded of their pothole moments. I want to encourage you not to allow the potholes of your life to stop your journey. God has made provisions for your potholes, and you don't have to wear out.

You can get back into alignment today and reconnect with your purpose in life.

We have all experienced deep, life-changing, discouraging potholes that left us bewildered. But God is faithful; He will not allow you to suffer anything you cannot handle. There is still a purpose for you and plenty of road left to drive. So don't give up. God is granting you another chance.

The next few chapters are crucial if this is what you desire. After going through my divorce, I thought my life was over. My name and reputation were destroyed, and the road was dark and lonely. I did not foresee any possibility of restoring my ministry; I felt doomed with no chance of recovery. My life was completely out of alignment, but I felt something deep inside calling me to press forward. I did not understand this feeling to try to succeed again, because I felt that God no longer had any use for me. I don't know if you can relate, but I felt my life was irreparable. When I looked around, all I saw was damage and wreckage. My wife was gone, my church was crushed, my children were hurting, and my haters were happy. People no longer saw me as that man of God who had it all together. For the first time in my ministry, I questioned God's ability to love me.

I know what you are thinking: how do you get realigned after life puts such devastating potholes in your path? It can be summed up in one word: purpose. The thing that called me out of my pothole of despair was that God still had a purpose for my life. Somewhere under all the ruin was a purpose that shouted, "God is not through with you!" I want you to catch this revelation. God is not through with you. Something good can come out of the worst moment of your life.

I know you are wondering, "How can I turn this situation around to work in my favor?" I am glad you asked. Allow me to tell you what I did.

First, I had to remember that the Bible is full of people who messed up their lives and experienced extreme failure, but God was able to put their lives back together, and He was willing to do the same for me. David failed horribly, Moses failed, Elijah failed, Peter failed, and just about every person you know has failed at something or in some way. But God was and is able to turn a mess into a miracle. I accepted that I was not the first person to have this experience and I would not be the last, and I had to depend on God to bring me through.

Here is my first piece of advice to you: do not see your situation as unique. This might be the first time you are experiencing something of this magnitude, but I promise it is not the first time anyone has faced it. Be encouraged and know that someone somewhere has gone through the same thing and come out on the other side. Trust me—life will get better.

Second, I learned to love myself again. When we encounter devastating moments in life, we often blame or punish ourselves. We degrade and belittle ourselves for behaving this way or for allowing others to treat us in this manner. We are left asking: Why did this happen? Why can't I get over it? Why am I like this? These questions render us helpless to change our circumstances because they dwell on the mistakes of the past. The one thing I have learned about the past is I can learn from it, but I cannot change it. Once we accept that we can't change the past, we are better qualified to learn from it and prevent it from resurfacing in the future. This aids in the process of loving yourself. As you release the past, you are postured to believe in yourself, and this opens the way to discover purpose for your life.

This step helps you realize that your current problem is someone's future solution. Once you come through your existing situation, your mission is to help others overcome and be victorious. Who is better to encourage someone who is struggling than someone who has successfully overcome the same struggle? The book you are reading came out of my pain, my struggle, and my disappointment in life. But as I learned to love myself again, my greatest purpose was awakened. Dreams and creativity began to flow out of me, and I took out my pen and started writing. The same is possible for you.

Third, shift from problem to purpose. Today, start moving away from your problem and into your purpose. You must resist the tendency to become depressed and discouraged. Your purpose is still deep inside you and will reactivate your drive to excel and succeed.

This was a pivotal part of my healing. Each day I would envision myself making a productive contribution to society. Yes, I am divorced; yes, I am a pastor; and yes, I disappointed a lot of people. But I still have a purpose on earth. I had to believe I was significant, or I would be doomed to wallow in my sorrow.

The same is true for you. Get up and realize your worth and your value. Once, when I was in Paris, I visited the Louvre and saw the Mona Lisa. While there, I a heard a story that someone had stolen the painting and scratched it, leaving a scar. I asked the guide if it affected the value of the painting, and her response was no—the painting increased in value. Isn't that something? The scratch increased the value of the art. The guide added that people would come from all around the world to see the scratch on the picture.

How much value have your scars added to your life?

Scripture

Jonah 2:1–3 (KJV): Then Jonah prayed unto the Lord his God out of the fish's belly, And said, I cried by reason of mine affliction unto the Lord, and he heard me; out of the belly of hell cried I, and thou heardest my voice. For thou hadst cast me into the deep, in the midst of the seas; and the floods compassed me about: all thy billows and thy waves passed over me.

Prayer

Father, as with Jonah, I cry out to You from the depths of my situation. I am confident that even though I have gotten off course, You still have a purpose for me. Father, I ask You to help me realign with Your plan for my life. Father, I ask that everything You have intended for me be clear so that I can't miss it. I fully surrender to You and ask that You guide me away from anything that impedes my pursuit of Your will. Father, help me take the proper steps and train my mind to stay focused on what is asked of me. I want to move forward in Jesus' name, amen.

Declaration

Father, I declare that I am complete in YOU. You have the best plan for my life, and I will fulfill Your perfect will for my life. Today, I am renewed, refreshed, and realigned with You, and I will not deviate from Your plans for my life. Yesterday is gone and behind me, and I choose to look to my future. I declare that I am on point, in place, and totally prepared for my next level. I decree that discouragement and failure will not be able to enter my mind or body. I am more than a conqueror. AMEN.

STEP 12
REHEARSE YOUR SUCCESS

"Do not allow your mind to imprison you in your recent dilemma."

"THANK GOD IT'S FRIDAY."

This term holds different meanings for different people. For some, it means the end of the workweek. For others, it is a time to hit the bars for happy hour and prepare to party for the rest of the weekend. But for me, after I had made a major change in my life, it was the time when I could work on my preaching skills. Every Friday night my housemates would go out and party at all the hot spots. They would normally leave around nine and would not return until two or three in the morning, leaving me with the house all to myself. As soon as they left, I would run upstairs, grab a sheet off my bed, and wrap it around myself to act as my clergy robe—in that day all preachers wore robes. I would proceed to my housemate's room, where I would use his dresser as a podium and his mirror so I could see myself. I would go through the entire introduction:

"Today, ladies and gentlemen, Reverend Chris Evans is here to share the word with us." I would stand up and say, "Take out your Bibles, and turn to" whatever my text was for the night. I would preach until I lost my voice or until I heard one of my housemates coming home.

What was I doing? I was rehearsing. I felt that God had a calling on my life, and one day I would preach in front of an audience. I remember the first time I got a speaking engagement. Hearing all the introductions, I felt like I had been there before. Actually, I had— every Friday night when my housemates would go out to party.

Once I went through my divorce, my life was filled with failure. I had failed God, myself, my family, my church, my mother, and my community. All I could think about was failure. I felt there was no chance for me ever to succeed at anything again. I believed that the only success I would have was past success. When you look at your life, how do you feel about your future? Whether you are the victim or the victimizer, your life can get better.

How do you rehearse success? You do it through visualization. When attempting to deal with devastating, life-altering problems, the mind becomes consumed by emotions of the moment. It can paint a picture of the future in response. Most of us are unfamiliar with techniques for resisting these negative emotions and believe that the pictures we see in our minds are accurate depictions of the future. I have heard of individuals who allowed their emotions to paint such pictures that suicide became their only escape.

Allow me to take a page from the United Negro College Fund: "A mind is a terrible thing to waste." Do not allow your mind to imprison you in your recent dilemma. Through the channels of your imagination, see your life as successful and thriving. When you feel like a failure, paint a picture. When you feel like you are worthless or unwanted, paint another picture. When you think you deserve to be mistreated and unappreciated, paint another picture. These pictures of a brighter, more promising future are called visualization.

This was the main factor that afforded me the opportunity to pursue another chance. I learned the power of visualization. Here is what I want you to do: paint a picture in your mind of the future you desire. Ignore where you are in life, what you have lost, or how you feel, and dream about another day that is coming. Visualize yourself as happy, healthy, and successful, and from this time forward, live as if you were in the picture. Every day I visualized myself speaking to people about the pain of failure and divorce. I visualized myself helping others not to make the same mistakes I made. I visualized myself as the greatest father in the world to my children. I visualized my church exploding, growing, and influencing my community for Christ. I took it one step further and visualized myself happily married and doing ministry together with my wife.

All of a sudden, my visualizations turned into a vision for my life. I sensed that something shifted. As my visualization continued, the manifestation was remarkable.

Why the change? Because I learned that manifestation is in direct correlation to visualization. In other words, whatever is happening or manifesting in you is a result of what you are focusing on or visualizing.

What are you rehearsing for? Remember, long before I was a speaking publicly I was rehearsing privately. Notice I did not say I was practicing, but rehearsing. To practice is to develop a skill; rehearsal is preparation for a show that is right around the corner. So, when the day came, I was already prepared to speak without fear or hesitation. See yourself accomplishing and achieving great things, and start rehearsing your success today.

Scripture

1 Samuel 17:34–36 (NASB): But David said to Saul, "Your servant was tending his father's sheep. When a lion or a bear came and took a lamb from the flock, I went out after him and attacked him, and rescued it from his mouth; and when he rose up against me, I seized him by his beard and struck him and killed him. Your servant has killed both the lion and the bear; and this uncircumcised Philistine will be like one of them, since he has taunted the armies of the living God."

Prayer

Heavenly Father, I know You have used various situations to prepare me for this moment. Help me to recall my victories in life. Help me to see every place and every time You caused me to succeed. Father, remind me of Your ability to protect and promote me. Grant me peace that passes all understanding, and give me assurance that the worst is behind and the best is ahead. Help me to stand in You and Your strength. I want to see every situation as a stepping stone and not a stumbling block. Help me to believe in myself as much as You do. Amen.

Declaration

Today, I expect to have victory as I have been prepped for this moment. I will recount my victories in life and allow them to strengthen me as I face this challenging season of my life. I will not be defeated today, but I will run and face my giants. Today, through You, I feel invincible, and I am determined to move forward with my life. Amen.

STEP 13
RESUME YOUR LIFE

"Good men start, but great men finish. This chapter in your life might be difficult, but be encouraged. It is not the end of the book."

"PLEASE DON'T LET THE BATS COME TONIGHT."

Years ago, when I first began my ministry, I was renting an old building called the Reunion Hall. It was used only once a week by a group of elderly women for a prayer meeting. Due to the limited use of the building, a group of bats took up residence. Occasionally, they would make an appearance to scare everybody half to death and then return to the attic.

I have always been a dreamer, even when I was in that old building, so I planned a prayer conference and invited a large number of people to attend. Well, it was my night to speak, and the place was packed with members and guests who had come to hear a word from the Lord. I prayed a lot that day, asking the Lord to bless the meeting, but mainly I prayed the bats would stay in the attic until the service was over. This was my first big gathering, and I really wanted everything to go well.

However, sometimes things don't go as planned, and we must learn how to roll with the punches. Right in the middle of my message, when I had everyone's attention, there came the bats. I could not believe my eyes. They were flying everywhere, and people were trying to keep their composure and contain their fear of the creepy creatures. It was extremely embarrassing, and I was coming unglued as I watched the men trying to kill the bats with brooms.

Eventually the men got them out, and the service continued. But how could I recover after such an interruption? Here is what I said: "Just like the bats caused a major distraction in our service, the devil wants to cause a major distraction in your life." When I said that, it was like I had planned the whole thing, and the audience immediately got the point. That night was one of the greatest messages I've ever preached, and many people received Christ as their Lord and Savior. Even though the message endured major interruptions, I had to use everything to my advantage. I had to pick up where I had left off.

There are times in life when undesirable things will show up at undesirable times and disturb our flow. We must learn how to resume our lives, our marriages, our finances, or our ministries in spite of the distractions. In other words, we must pick up where we left off before the interruption came. None of us will live without untimely, inconveniencing situations that force us to readjust our plans. What has come into your life that has caused emotional discomfort and distress, forcing you to go a different route? What has come that you thought you would never have to deal with? An even better question is: how do you handle these moments and resume your life?

First, do not live in denial. I have met so many people who attempt to deal with stressful moments in their lives by acting like nothing is happening. The quicker you face these moments, the quicker you can fix them. Whether you like it or not, this situation has found its way to your address and will not leave simply because you act like it's not there. So, don't deny it, just deal with it.

We could have acted, all we wanted, as if those bats were not in the room, and they would have continued to interfere with the church service. The same is true for you. Your life will get better the day you come out of denial and say, "I have to get rid of these bats." Take a minute and ask God to help you face what is currently happening in your life.

Second, depend on God to help you through this moment. In the toughest moments of our lives, God is always there. We struggle with believing He is aware of our needs, our problems, and our pains. But He is so aware of where you are and what you are going through. In times like these, we must trust God and know that this, too, will pass. We must depend on God for His peace, His strength, and His wisdom.

THE PEACE OF GOD

His peace passes all understanding. There are times when we don't understand, and we must rely on God's peace to calm the stormy seas of life. We can have peace when we know that He loves us and has planned the best for us, and even when it does not look like He is working on our behalf. During these times, we must trust the faithfulness of God and know that He is with us. How do we walk in God's peace? By training our minds to think on the right things.

> *Philippians 4:8 (KJV): Finally, brethren, whatsoever things are true, whatsoever things are honest, whatsoever things are just, whatsoever things are pure, whatsoever things are lovely, whatsoever things are of good report; if there be any virtue, and if there be any praise, think on these things.*

> *Philippians 4:9B (KJV): And the God of peace shall be with you.*

I encourage you to set your mind on good things, on the future, and on the victory that this moment will breed.

THE STRENGTH OF GOD

There are times when we face situations that are greater than our strength, and we have to trust in the Lord for His strength. The Bible tells the story of David, who returned from battle and found that his camp had been burned and his family and the families of his soldiers had been taken captive. David was so hurt by the siege that he and his soldiers wailed until they had no more strength.

David did an amazing thing at one of the weakest times in his life. The Bible says he encouraged himself in the Lord (1 Samuel 30:6, KJV). David realized that although he was weak, God was still strong. Perhaps you have lost something that was valuable to you, and it is difficult to find the strength you need to carry on. This is the perfect time to trust that God has enough strength for the both of you.

Job 39:11A (KJV) states: "Wilt thou trust him, because his strength is great?" His grace is sufficient. Why don't you lift your hands and encourage yourself in the Lord and know that God has your back?

THE WISDOM OF GOD

What do you do when you don't know what to do? In my life and ministry, there have been times when I didn't know what to do or where to turn for help. I learned that in every situation of my life, the word of God held the keys that would help me transcend the season. The apostle Paul, in Ephesians 3:10 (KJV), called it "the manifold wisdom of God," which means God's wisdom is unsearchable and unlimited. He knows all and knows how to handle every situation in life before it ever occurs.

I know you are wondering how to access this wisdom. It's simple. According to James 1:5 (KJV): "If any of you lack wisdom, let him ask of God, that giveth to all men liberally, and upbraideth not; and it shall be given him." That's right—you ask God to show you how to get through this setback, and He will guide and lead you. Isn't that amazing? All you have to do is ask Him to give you wisdom.

As we close this book, I want you to create a new habit of depending on God's peace, God's strength, and God's wisdom to aid you when there are insurmountable odds. Today, I want you to resume your life by knowing that God is with you, and every test leads to a testimony. Someone will benefit from this chapter of your life, but be encouraged because it is not the end of the book. Your best days are still ahead.

Scripture

Isaiah 38:5 (NIV): "Go and tell Hezekiah, 'This is what the Lord, the God of your father David, says: I have heard your prayer and have seen your tears; I will add fifteen years to your life.'"

Prayer

Father, thank You that I have more living to do. I ask You to help me to take advantage of every day and make the most of it. Father, help and grant me the strength to go on from all past hurts, failures, and disappointments. Restore to me the joy of life and thrill of living a fulfilling and exciting life. Help me overcome anything that attempts to steal my joy and zest for life. Thank You that I feel alive again; therefore, help me not look back over the failures of yesterday. I receive that You have added to my life, and I celebrate who I am and where I am headed. Amen.

Declaration

I declare that today will be different from any other day of my life. I will walk with a new restored sense of confidence. Today, I am fully convinced that things are turning in my favor and that I will be able to handle whatever comes my way. I am anxiously anticipating my next level, and I have a positive outlook on life. Today, I attempt new things and reach for the deepest dreams and desires of my heart. Today will be an awesome day.

STEP 14
REMAIN DILIGENT

"Another chance in life is possible if you are willing to remain diligent."

"THAT CAN'T BE WHO I THINK IT IS."

Have you ever known someone who was overweight or extremely thin, and you saw them years later and they were completely the opposite of how you remembered them? A couple of days ago, I was in the gym and I saw this gentleman I had not seen in about fifteen years. As I walked past him, he said, "Pastor Evans." I looked, and he said, "I know you don't recognize me."

"I don't," I replied.

He said, "It's me" and stated his name.

I could not believe what was before my eyes. I said, "Man, I would not have recognized you in a million years." He looked completely different. The last time I had seen him, he'd been about four hundred pounds and totally out of shape. Now he was a lean, 185 pounds of pure muscle. It was absolutely incredible to witness such a remarkable feat. This guy had lost more than two hundred pounds and looked ten years younger.

Immediately I started asking him questions to see how he had pulled this off. After much dialogue, he gave me the secret to his success. He said, "I decided to be diligent and faithful to my eating and workout program." This triggered something in me because I had been going to the gym off and on for over a year and a half, but I did not have the kind of results he had. What was the difference between us? Well, for one, he had a completely sculpted body, but the main difference was his diligence. That's the last piece of the puzzle. Some things won't change in your life without a commitment to diligently practicing the principles and habits that will produce the results you desire.

What is diligence? It is a constant effort to accomplish something or to be attentive and persistent in doing anything. Another chance in life is possible if you are willing to remain diligent. What am I saying? In order to maximize all the principles within this book, you must head in the right direction and keep going. It does not matter if you are the wounded or the offender; life can change for you if you are courageous enough to find out what is right and do it consistently for the rest of your life.

Another definition of diligent is knowing what to do and when to do it, and doing it over an extended period of time. Nothing in your life will improve as long as you have an on-again, off-again mentality. What you desire is possible, but you must be diligent and persistently charge ahead and watch things materialize right before your eyes. After you finish this book, I challenge you to remove the following phrases from your speech:

- I quit.
- I can't.
- It's too hard.
- It's impossible.
- It's not for me.
- Why try?
- I will only fail again.
- I will never . . .

When you diligently put into action the things you have learned in this book, your life with dramatically change for the better. You will feel better about yourself and your future. But you must guard against setbacks and relapses. I have discovered that whatever you practice, negative or positive, will produce results. Make up your mind today to get focused, and prepare for your life to soar to heights beyond your wildest imagination. This is all possible because you decided not to get trapped in the moment of your misery or your mistakes.

You are a special breed and rank among an elite group of individuals who realize that life is not over. You have been granted another chance. Believe it, seize it, and you will achieve it. And one day soon, someone will look at you and not recognize you because you will look nothing like this current moment in your life. I am so excited for you.

Scripture

Proverbs 13:4 (ESV): The soul of the sluggard craves and gets nothing, while the soul of the diligent is richly supplied.

Prayer

Father, I ask for a strong desire to be excellent. I pray that You will give me the ability to work to the best of my ability. I know that my time and energy are very precious in every field I take up in life, so Father, bless me to stay strong, even when the world around me has so many distractions. I thank You for giving me the desire to fulfill Your purpose for me. With You, I know I can and will accomplish my goals and plans for my life. Amen.

Declaration

I declare I will be proactive and not reactive. I will go after life and respond positively to the challenges I will face. Each day I will work diligently and not waste time or effort on things that are unfruitful and unproductive. I will be fruitful and productive. I declare I have the stamina and the strength to complete every task that is before me. This day, I will not waste time but will leverage my time and talents to advance my life. Amen.

CONCLUSION

"This is my hope for you. I pray that something I said has caused a shift in your life."

I remember when I first got the idea to write this book, it was difficult to recall incidents that I wished to forget. However, now that I am on the other side of the storm, I can say I have gone from bad to better.

This is my hope for you. I pray that something I've said has caused a shift in your life. Every life will have its fair share of pain and problems, but know there is light at the end of the tunnel. You, too, will realize what I came to realize…that regardless of where you are or what negative set of circumstances you encounter—regardless of what you have lost, regardless of what devastating blow you have endued, regardless of who has left you, hurt you, abused you, or passed away before you—you are still here, and you have a lot of living to do.

I opened this book by saying I know how you feel, and maybe our roads are somewhat different, but pain is pain, and disappointment is disappointment. So trust me when I say life can and will get better. Let me be the first to say you have plenty to live for and plenty of living to do. Think about it: a couple moments ago I was in a smelly hotel room and now I'm an author. Trust that you have plenty of living left to do. Here's the problem: I know something that you don't know.

First, I know you are capable of handling much more than you are aware of. As you are applying the steps of this book, you will tap in to an inner strength you didn't realize you had. You will discover courage to face and fight life's oppositions. In the days ahead, what was so tough to handle and possibly drove you crazy will lose its ability to influence and affect your emotions. You are tougher and stronger than you know.

I once heard a story of a woman who married her high school sweetheart and they had the best marriage two humans could possibly have. This darling woman had saved herself sexually for him, and him for her. They both had promising careers and two intelligent children. Then the unthinkable happened. She received a knock at the door, and she opened it to find a state police officer standing on the other side. He informed her that her husband had been killed in a head-on collision. She was completely devastated. Her husband was her life and the father of her children. She wrestled with suicide but quickly abandoned the thought as she envisioned her children without both parents. But how could she go on? This man was her everything. After grieving, she came to the conclusion that she was still alive. Today, she is remarried to another wonderful man and is living the life she dreamed of. How did she do it? She found a strength she didn't know she had. The same is true for you, and you have more than you know.

Second, your current storm is your future story. Growing up, I always loved it when my mother would read me a bedtime story. My favorite was "The Three Little Pigs." I'm sure you know the story. But in case you've never heard it, allow me to share the main points. This story tells of these three pigs who built three houses out of three different materials—one out of straw, one out of sticks, and one out of bricks. Their archrival was this mean wolf who would attempt to blow their houses down. The wolf was successful on the first two attempts. He destroyed the house made of straw and of sticks but met his match when he attempted to ruin the house of bricks. When he tried to blow it down, this house was strong enough to resist the force of his wind. As a child, I learned two things: that in life I would encounter a wolf, and to build my house out of brick.

You might not realize this, but our struggles are nothing but stories in the making. What you are facing now will become a life lesson for someone else later. When I was going through my storm, I had to draw on the survival stories of others to get me through. Today, my past struggle has become a book to tell the world that you can get another chance. I don't know if your story will be a book or a movie, but I promise you it needs to be told. Maybe in the grocery store, between the T-bone steaks and boneless chicken breasts, there will be someone who is at the end of their rope. Maybe at the car wash, the mall, a restaurant, the doctor's office . . . I don't know where, but your struggle will become a great story to help someone get through their struggle.

Last but not least, I know that it will make sense later. When I was a child and had to deal with something tough, my grandmother would say, "You will understand it better by and by." I never could grasp the revelation of this cliché. Years later, I shared a secret with a gentlemen I assumed to be a close friend. The secret didn't stay put with him and he shared it with individuals he knew would spread it. Embarrassed, hurt, and confused, I could not understand why someone would betray me this way, considering he was well aware of the gravity of this situation. I didn't understand it then, but I understand it now. That day life was teaching me some valuable lessons. These lessons I utilize to this day. One, friendships are built over time. Two, there are some things you must keep to yourself. I didn't, and in a crash course in friendship, life was teaching me to choose my friends carefully and wisely.

There are many occasions in life that cause you to look and say, "That's what it meant." Sometimes we learn the meaning of the pain later on down the road. Someone once said, "We will look back on this and laugh." Well, I am not sure if this is true in every case because some things were not funny then, and they are not funny now. But I do believe we can look back and learn. We should always learn from our mistakes, shortcomings, and disappointments. As strange as it may sound, there is a lesson to learn from where you are right now. I know you just want out and want your life to flow as usual. But for some reason, this has come your way, and I don't know why, and I don't know why now. So I guess, like my grandmother said, "Some things we will understand better by and by."

Made in the USA
Middletown, DE
15 August 2018